SOURDOUGH SECRETS...
REVEALED!

by

Ray Templeton

Sourdough Secrets... Revealed!

Authored by Ray Templeton

Edited by S. E. Thomas

Published by The Dramatic Pen Press, L.L.C.

Lolo, Montana

ISBN-10: 0692391630
ISBN-13: 978-0692391631

Table of Contents

Introduction:
Welcome to Idaho Sourdough!

If you are reading this, I bet you love sourdough bread, biscuits, pancakes, waffles, and other sourdough baked goods. I'm also willing to bet that you have tried to create your own sourdough bread sometime in the past and you didn't have great success with your sourdough attempts. Am I right or am I right? Sometimes it seems like it is impossible to unlock the secrets of sourdough and many of the people who have discovered the secrets of success are unwilling to share that information with beginners. They seem to forget that, at some time in the past, they were beginners, too. The purpose of this book is to show you how to successfully make a sourdough starter, nurture it allowing it to proliferate, and use it to create good sourdough bread. Once you get the hang of manipulating a sourdough starter using some of the secrets of sourdough, you will be able to move forward in your sourdough knowledge and create your own recipes for wonderful sourdough bread and other sourdough treats.

Happy Baking,

Ray Templeton

PART I

Getting Started

Chapter One:
Making the Starter

First, I want to tell you the three most important words you need to understand to make great sourdough bread. Those three words are: PATIENCE, PATIENCE, and PATIENCE! In case you didn't catch that, it is imperative that you exercise patience when working with sourdough. I know, I know… how can you exercise patience when you can hardly wait to spread some butter on that hot-out-of-the-oven sourdough bread you are going to make and enjoy that wonderful taste that arouses your senses? But to be truly successful with sourdough, you must have patience. Going hand-in-hand with patience is the phrase; "haste makes waste." The death blow to your sourdough project will be when you think to yourself, "I think I can do this faster by…." Don't be tempted to take shortcuts. Sourdough takes having a plan and planning ahead. The actual time spent working on your sourdough project is negligible compared to the time waiting for your starter to be ready to use and the rising times involved before you actually put your bread into the oven.

To assure your success with your first sourdough bread project, please follow the instructions and observe the times allotted for starter development and dough rising. These times are not set in concrete. Sourdough rising times can vary quite a bit with yeast strain types, proofing area temperatures, and the recipes being used. Once you have several successful projects under your belt, you can start to experiment with your own ideas and methods. There are many fancy and technical terms used in sourdough that we will discuss in this book—after you have successfully baked and consumed your first loaf of sourdough bread.

Sourdough baking isn't rocket science... unless you want it to be. You can make it as simple or as complex as you would like it to be in your future projects. For now, let's make this first project as easy as possible. I want your first project to be a smashing success so that you will gain confidence and become increasingly excited about sourdough. When your friends and family rave about your sourdough bread, you'll be hooked on sourdough for life.

Let's talk about the ingredients and equipment you'll be using in making sourdough. The first ingredient is water.

Water

This is very important. You can**not** use chlorinated water with sourdough. The chlorine will kill the yeast. I'm lucky—I live out in the sticks of northern Idaho and have my own well. Our well water is awesome. But if you live in the big city or even a medium sized city, you are on city water. City water is almost always chlorinated. Many cities' water is fluorinated as well. These additives to city water are there to kill the "bad" bugs that live in the water. The additives keep the water from becoming contaminated. Unfortunately, the additives to city water which kill the "bad" bugs also kill the "good" bugs. In our case, that means the yeast. So, if you don't have a source of water that is not chlorinated, please use bottled water. There are also fancy water filtered pitchers on the market. If you are planning to use the water from one of these pitchers, please make sure it filters chlorine from the water.

Flour

As you gain more knowledge and experience with sourdough, you will want to learn about all the different kinds of flour and how they influence your sourdough baking. For your first project, you will be using Unbleached All-Purpose White Flour. Please use fresh, quality flour for your starter and bread.

Yeast

Yeast is composed of the little critters that make your bread rise. I'm not going to go into a big dissertation at this point, but I want to give you a little background on yeast. Back in the dark ages, when I was in school, they didn't actually know if yeast was a plant or an animal. It displayed characteristics of both a plant and an animal. Over time, they have determined that it is a fungus. Yeast eats sugar and can convert starch to sugar so it can consume it. It likes simple sugars and can't deal well with complex sugars. Its waste products are CO_2 and alcohol. The CO_2 (carbon dioxide) is what makes the bread rise. These little critters are tough in some ways and fragile in other ways. They are most fragile in their ability to handle high temperatures. They die at 138° F. This is important to know, as most sourdough starter recipes and bread recipes call for "warm" water. If your "warm" water is over 138° F, you've killed your yeast. This is most likely the reason for so many people failing in their first sourdough-making attempt (along with using chlorinated water.) Their "warm" water was too hot and they killed their yeast.

While our main yeast contribution with sourdough is wild yeast, you will also occasionally be using commercial yeast in some of your bread recipes. I will give you a choice about your first loaf. You can create bread with only wild yeast — a true sourdough bread, or you can create an improved sourdough bread that contains some commercial yeast and other ingredients besides the flour, water, and salt that all wild yeast bread uses. In fact, I will give you several choices when that time comes. But back to commercial yeast. There are several different kinds of commercial yeast on your grocery shelf — regular yeast, rapid-rise yeast, and instant yeast. You may have to "start" or "proof" regular yeast and rapid-rise yeast before you add them to your ingredients, but modern commercial yeast can generally be used without proofing. I use instant yeast.

Make sure your yeast is viable, meaning that it is alive. The easiest way to do this is to add some yeast to some warm (80-85° F) water mixed with a little sugar. In a few minutes, your mixture should start bubbling and foaming. This assures that your yeast is usable.

Equipment

First, you will need a large glass or plastic mixing bowl. I have used both glass and plastic—but prefer glass. The ones in the picture below are both 6 quarts in size. This size allows for approximately 4 cups of flour, 2 cups of water, and enough room for the expansion of the rising starter and/or bread dough.

You'll also need typical kitchen tools — mixing spoons, measuring cups, spoons, etc.

I <u>highly recommend</u> getting an instant-read, digital thermometer. I use mine to check the temperature of the area I choose for rising, the temperature of the "warm" water I use with my starters, and to check the internal temperature of my bread at the end of its baking time.

Mixer

While you can knead your bread by hand, it helps to have a stand mixer with a dough hook to knead your bread dough. I like to do the last kneading by hand, even though I use my stand mixer to do most of the early kneading.

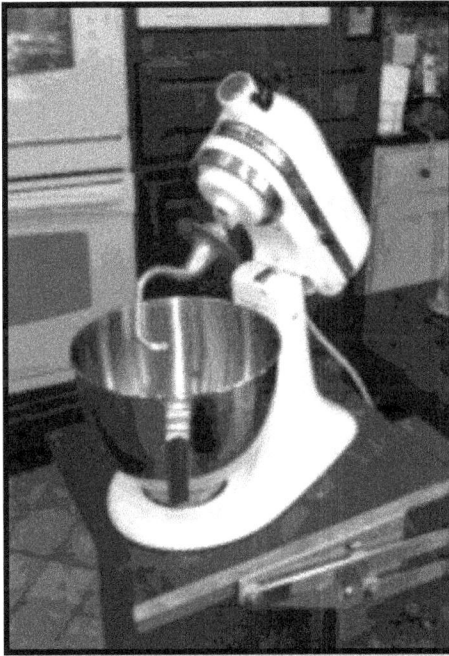

Starter Storage

You will need some way to store your starter in the refrigerator between bread making projects. The best and easiest storage incorporates the use of wide mouth, 1 quart canning jars. Do not screw down the lid too tightly—just loosely.

Spray Bottle

You will need a spray bottle so that you can spray water on your sourdough loaf just before you put it in the oven to bake. This helps the crust to bake and brown properly. I stole my little spray bottle from a haircut kit (I really don't need much in the way of haircuts any more), but any spray bottle will work. Most have a nozzle adjustment so you can make the spray very fine.

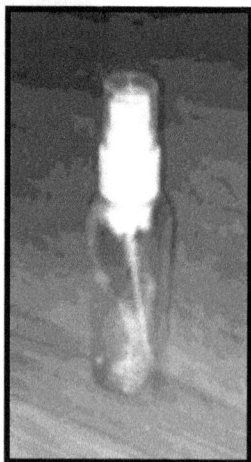

<u>Baking Pans</u>

While most people just place their sourdough loaf on a sheet pan or baking stone, many people like putting their sourdough loaf in a covered baking pan. Dutch Ovens are great for this, but, unless you already have one on hand and it is the right size for baking sourdough bread, they are quite expensive to purchase just for baking sourdough bread. I have used my all-metal cookware, which is adequate.

Though we are used to seeing sourdough bread in round loaves, oblong loaves, and long loaves, we may find it easier and more convenient to use a regular loaf pan.

Proofing & Rising Area

It is important to find an area where you can put your starter as you revive it and your bread dough to let it rise, which is a fairly consistent 70–75°F. Before I built a "proofing box" to serve this requirement, I used an end table in our family room. I recorded the temperature on that end table over several days, and it was always between 70°F and 74°F. Unfortunately, my wife got tired of seeing bowls of sourdough starter fermenting in her family room. This, and the ability to accurately control the temperature of the area where I put my starters and dough, was a catalyst to my building of a proofing box. I talk more about a proofing box in Part II of this book.

Now it is time to prepare your starter. Often, you can acquire a starter sample from a friend or a company. (See Index Two: Starters and Additional Resources.) However, do not fear! As promised, this book provides directions for creating your own starter at home. If you prefer to go that route first, skip to Part II of this book. In Chapter Twelve: Creating Your Own Starter, I provide step-by-step instructions to do just that. However, these first set of instructions are for using a pre-made starter. The process is the same if you are using a starter from someone else or a starter you created from scratch. Whichever route you choose, just follow the instructions and you'll be enjoying your first loaf of sourdough bread before you know it.

Chapter Two:
Starter Instructions

These instructions are for reviving, propagating, and using the resultant starter (yeast culture) to create sourdough bread, starting with the yeast culture you purchased or created using the instructions provided in Chapter Twelve of this book. Pay attention to the techniques used to take your original yeast culture to your final loaf of sourdough bread, as these techniques are fairly constant for working with any yeast culture.

Before we get started, I just want to remind you about working with sourdough. Be sure to clean your bowls, tools, and starter jars as soon as possible after taking the sourdough out of them or after using them. Once dry, sourdough starter is like concrete. Also remember, the times given for proofing and rising are estimates. Your times may vary. Over time, you will get an idea of what times your starter needs to be ready or how long it will take your bread to rise so that it is ready to bake. All wild yeast breads will take considerably longer than recipes using some commercial yeast in them.

Likely, you will have preserved whatever starter sample you will be using in the refrigerator, if you weren't going to start your sourdough starter right away. Like I said in the introduction, sourdough requires you to plan ahead. Once you have read this booklet and are ready to actually start reviving your culture, take it out of the refrigerator and allow it to come to "room temperature" — around 70°F.

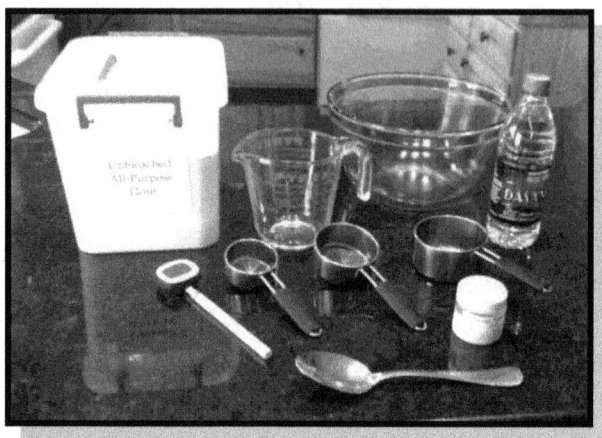

As your culture is warming to room temperature, make sure you have all the other items needed to get your culture up and running.

You will need a large glass or plastic bowl. We have several 5-6 quart glass bowls we like to use. You will also need Unbleached All-Purpose White Flour and water. Since we live out in the sticks of northern Idaho, we have our own well and our water works just fine right out of the tap. But if you live in a larger city and are on a city water system, your tap water most likely has chlorine and/or fluoride in it. Do not use chlorinated water as this will kill the yeast. If you are on city water, you will need to use non-chlorinated bottled water. Pour some bottled water into a glass measuring cup and use a microwave to warm the water to around 85-90°F. Use your instant-read digital thermometer to check the water temperature.

You also need to find an area in your home that maintains a fairly consistent temperature of around 70-75°F. This could take some time to find as the temperature can change over a 24 hour period. If you fall in love with sourdough and want to continue to make sourdough on a regular basis, you will want to construct a "proofing box" to use in the future. But at this time, just try to find an area in your home that stays around 70-75°F.

You will also need two (2) 1 quart jars to store your starter in — one for your "safety net" culture and the other for your "working" culture.

If you are going to use loaf pans or a Dutch oven to bake your first loaf (loaves) in, be sure they are ready. You won't need them immediately, but you will need them soon.

Once you have all the items ready and your starter culture is at room temperature, you're ready to go. I have numbered the steps to make them easier to follow.

1. The type of starter you have will determine how you proceed. If you have purchased a starter that is in dry form, follow the instructions that were included with the starter. If you have a liquid starter you received from another baker, you will need at least 2 tablespoons of the starter in the bowl before proceeding to instruction #2.

2. Add ¾ cup of the warm (80-85°F) water to the bowl. Stir until the starter has combined with the water.

Add 1 cup of Unbleached All-Purpose White Flour and mix until smooth.

3. Cover bowl with plastic wrap and place in the spot you found that is a consistent 70-75°F.

Let it rest there for 8–12 hours. After 8–12 hours*, the starter should be bubbly.

After 4 Hours	After 7 Hours	After 9 Hours

4. Stir the starter. Mix in ¾ cup lukewarm water (80–85°F) and 1 cup flour. The starter will be like pancake batter. Cover the bowl with plastic wrap and let sit for around 4-6 hours for this 2nd Proof. The starter will, <u>once again</u>, become bubbly.

5. Stir the starter and divide it in half. Place one half of the starter into one of the jars. Label this jar as your original culture. This is a "fall-back-on" safety net. If disaster strikes, and you lose your working starter, you can come back to this culture and revive it.

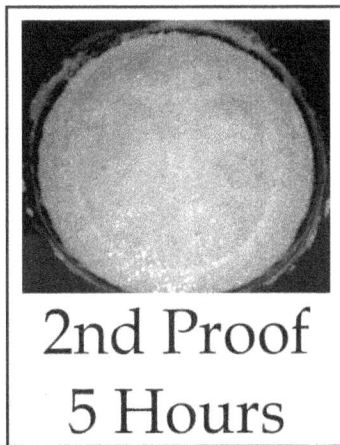

2nd Proof
5 Hours

6. "Feed" the remaining half with ¾ cup lukewarm water (80–85°F) and 1 cup of flour. The starter will be thick to start—stir until smooth.

7. Cover the bowl with plastic wrap and let sit for around 4-6 hours. The starter should, once again, become bubbly. (See images above for reference.)

8. Stir down the starter. If you are ready to make bread right now, take 1 cup of starter out of the bowl and put in the mixer's bowl.

9. Feed the left over starter with ¾ cup warm (80-85°F) water and 1 cup of flour. Mix until smooth. Cover and let stand in your 70°F area for 4-6 hours, or until it is bubbly. (See images above for reference.)

10. Stir the starter and place into the other 1 qt. jar. Make sure that your jar is clean. Put the lid on the jar and make it just loose. This is your "working" culture.

11. Label your jar lid with the name of your starter and the date you put it into the jar. Place the jar in the refrigerator until you are ready to make bread again.

Note: Read the section on taking the refrigerated starter and making it ready to make more bread. From this point on, when you feed your starter, if you are not making bread, you discard the cup of starter you take out of your working culture. This gives the yeast fresh flour to process.

Chapter Three:
Maintaining Your Starter in the Refrigerator

If you don't use your starter once in a week's time to create a sourdough recipe, it is a good idea to feed your starter, even if you aren't going to use it in a recipe. If you forget and don't feed it, don't despair — all is not lost.

According to what strain of yeast your starter is created from, you may have a little or a lot of fluid collected on the top of your starter. This fluid could be green, gray, or brown.

This is OK — the fluid is just the alcohol bi-product from the fermenting yeast. If the fluid is kind of pink or smells bad — not just tangy or like alcohol, your starter may be contaminated. At this point in your sourdough education, it is probably best to just discard this starter and fall back on your "back-up" starter from earlier in the process. (In Chapter Six, I tell you how to "wash" your starter. The method I describe there can sometimes recover your contaminated starter back to a viable starter.)

1. Stir this fluid back into the starter until blended and smooth. Discard 1 cup of the starter. Now feed the starter in the normal method — ¾ cup of lukewarm (80-85°F) water and 1 cup of Unbleached All-Purpose Flour.

2. Stir until smooth, place in your clean jar, and place back in the refrigerator. No need to wait for it to get bubbly, unless you are planning to use it in a recipe right away.

Chapter Four:
Using the Starter in a Recipe

Now you have a sourdough starter ready to be used in a recipe. "How do I use the stuff in the jar to make sourdough bread?" you may ask. I'm glad you asked. This is what you do.

Many recipes call for a "fed" starter. To create a fed starter, take your starter out of the refrigerator and allow it to reach room temperature. Stir the starter and discard 1 cup of the starter. Or, instead of throwing it out, you could give this starter to a friend so they can have their own sourdough starter, or you could use this cup of starter to make some sourdough pancakes or waffles. There are recipes later in this book that teach you how to make these items. It is also a good idea to save this portion of starter as a "back-up" (if you don't already have a back-up starter) in case some kind of disaster occurs and you lose the starter you are working with at this point. I'll talk more about this later.

To the remaining starter, add ¾ cup of lukewarm water and 1 cup of flour. Stir until smooth, cover with plastic wrap, and let sit for 4-12 hours. The longer your starter has been in the refrigerator, the longer it will take for it to become bubbly. Once it is bubbly, it has become a "fed" starter and is ready to use in a recipe.

Take the amount of starter you need in your recipe, usually 1 cup, out of the bowl. Feed the remaining starter with ¾ cup lukewarm water and 1 cup of flour. Stir until smooth. Cover with plastic wrap and let sit for around 4 hours until bubbly. Stir down the starter and put it back in its jar (after you have washed the jar, of course). Place it in the refrigerator until you are ready to use it in your next sourdough recipe.

By now, you are seeing the "pattern" for feeding and using your starter. We will explain later why we divide the starter in half and discard some of the starter. When I started working with sourdough, I hated to throw away starter and tried to save it. Before long, I had starter coming out of my ears. You'll find the happy medium of having sourdough starter and room left in your refrigerator for food somewhere along the way.

Chapter Five:
Your First Loaf of Sourdough Bread

Now comes the fun. You've revived the starter sample you purchased or created. You've fed it and brought it to the point that it is ready to use for making bread. Proper care of this starter can keep you in sourdough bread for a lifetime. Sourdough starters have been passed down through generations. They have even been left in wills. I created my starter from wild yeast in the air of the Idaho Palouse.

For your first sourdough bread, I will give you the choice between several different bread recipes — the Old Prospector's Sourdough Bread recipe creates a pure sourdough loaf (no added commercial yeast in this recipe) just like the old prospectors made. The Improved All-Wild-Yeast Sourdough Bread recipe is an all-wild-yeast recipe that contains some additional ingredients to improve the taste. And the Improved Sourdough Bread recipe creates an improved sourdough bread that contains additional ingredients, including some commercial yeast. With the all-wild-yeast sourdough recipes, the rising times will be longer — considerably longer. With sourdough, longer is generally better. The slower your sourdough rises, the better flavor it will have. The improved sourdough recipe adds some commercial yeast and therefore reduces rising times. It is also less critical with its rising times; there is some flexibility in the times. Once again, it's your choice.

There are hundreds of recipes for sourdough out there. Feel free to try any or all of these once you have made your first loaf. I really want you to make one of the following recipes and to follow the instructions exactly. I want you to be totally successful in this first sourdough project. Once you know that you can do it, then start playing around with other recipes.

Old Prospector's Sourdough Bread is an all-wild-yeast recipe and is quite simple. The ingredients are: starter, water, salt, and flour.

That's it. Later in this book you will find recipes for several different sizes of loaves. For your first loaf, if you choose to make this recipe, use this small loaf recipe.

Old Prospector's Sourdough Bread

Ingredients

- 1 cup of your starter
- 1 cup of water
- 1 teaspoon salt
- 3½ cups Unbleached All-Purpose White Flour

Directions

1. Place your starter into a bowl. Add water and salt into the starter and mix.

2. Add flour 1 cup at a time until dough is too stiff to stir by hand.

3. If you are hand kneading, turn dough onto a floured board and knead in remaining flour until dough is smooth. Knead for 20 minutes. Yeah, I know, that's a lot of kneading by hand and that's why I recommend using a stand mixer with a dough hook.

4. If you are using a mixer with a dough hook, move dough into mixer's bowl and add the remaining flour a half a cup at a time. Once all the ingredients are combined, knead on the second speed for 15 minutes. <u>Attention!</u> If you decided to not follow my instructions and chose to make a large or extra-large loaf, and you are using a standard size stand mixer, the dough will climb up the dough hook and try to

infiltrate the planetary gears of your mixer. You have been warned.

5. Take a large bowl—large enough to hold about 4 times the mass of your sourdough as it is right now. Pour some olive oil into the bowl and use a paper towel to coat the inside of the bowl. You want it to be wet with oil.

6. Take the dough out of the mixer bowl, or from your kneading board, and put it into the oiled bowl. Move it around in the bowl and turn it over. Make sure that the dough is coated with olive oil.

7. Place plastic wrap over the bowl and set the bowl in your rising area. Whenever I have a bowl that has plastic wrap on it, I use a felt tip pen to write on the plastic reminding me what's in the bowl and what time I put it in the bowl.

8. Let the dough proof (rise) for 8–12 hours*. The dough will double in size. If your dough rises to double its original size before 8 hours, great. Proceed with the next step. Note the plastic in the next photo; the CO_2 gas from the yeast has caused it to expand.

9. After the dough has doubled in size, turn the dough onto a floured board. Fold the dough a couple of times. Cover the dough with plastic (just lay plastic wrap on top of the dough), and let stand (rest) for 30 minutes.

10. If the dough pretty much keeps its shape, you're good. If the dough seems to collapse or flatten out, knead in some additional flour (2–4 tablespoons) before shaping.

11. Now it is time to shape the dough. Shaping is more important than you would think. Most people, with their first loaf, will just make a round ball of the dough. I usually will fold the

loaf both vertically and horizontally and put any seams on the bottom of the loaf.

12. Place the loaf on a baking sheet, either greased or with parchment paper, or in a Dutch oven, or a sauce pan (all metal — no plastic handles allowed). Cover with plastic wrap and let rise at room temperature or a little higher — 75-80°F — for 2–4 hours, or until doubled in size.

13. Use a razor blade to slash the top of the dough — two slashes will be fine. Spray (my suggestion), or gently brush loaf with olive oil. Place loaf into a COOL oven. Turn on oven and set to 375°F. Bake for 70 minutes.

Note: If you are baking your bread in a covered pan, such as a Dutch oven, you're fine. Your sourdough loaf will be done in 70 minutes. Take the lid off around ten (10) minutes before it is supposed to be done. If the top isn't brown enough, leave the lid off for the last ten (10) minutes.

If you are baking your bread on a sheet pan or stone, use your spray bottle to lightly spray the top of the loaf. Place a shallow bowl on the bottom rack of the oven and fill it with hot water. Watch the oven temperature. When it reaches 212°F, open the oven door and spray a fine mist into the oven. If you do not have a digital readout on your oven for temperature, wait ten (10) minutes for this first spray. Do this again in five (5) minutes. Do it again in another five (5) minutes. Watch your loaf. If it starts to get too brown before the 70 minutes are up, lay some aluminum foil over the loaf.

The improved All-Wild-Yeast Sourdough Bread recipe is also simple, but adds a few additional ingredients.

* Rising times are approximates.

Comments: This bread is a basic sourdough bread. It is just like what the old prospectors baked while gold mining. Sometime in your baking adventures, you should make this recipe. It may not be the best recipe for your first loaf. The rising times are long and it is critical that, once your dough has doubled in size, you don't let it rise a lot longer. If you let it rise considerably longer than doubling in size, it may not have a lot left for the actual loaf rising. It is not a complex bread, either in ingredients or in taste.

Improved All-Wild-Yeast Sourdough Bread

This recipe calls for two (2) cups of starter. To get two (2) cups of starter to make your bread, take the one (1) cup of starter you would normally put in the mixer's bowl and put it into a separate bowl. Feed this starter with ¾ cup warm water and 1 cup of Unbleached All-Purpose Flour. Stir until smooth, cover with plastic and let it proof for 3-4 hours. Now you have two (2) cups of starter ready to make your bread.

Ingredients

- 2 cups fresh starter
- 1 cup warm water
- 2 tablespoons sugar
- 1 teaspoon salt
- 4 tablespoons dry milk powder
- 2 tablespoons olive oil
- 4-6 cups bread flour (Note that this recipe uses BREAD flour.
- Melted butter (Optional)

Directions

1. Combine and mix together starter, water, sugar, and dry milk.

2. Place dough hook on stand mixer and mix. Add salt, oil, and 3 cups of bread flour. Knead on first speed until ingredients are mixed. Add

additional flour and knead on speed 2 or 3 until dough ball forms. Knead for an additional 5-10 minutes.

3. Place dough in an olive oil coated bowl, cover with plastic, and let rise until doubled in size.

4. Punch down; let rest 15 minutes.

5. Shape into two (2) loaves and place on parchment covered sheet pan, on a baking stone, or in loaf pans.

6. Spray with olive oil, cover with plastic, and let rise until doubled in size.

7. Slash with floured razor blade. (For a softer crust, brush tops with melted butter.)

8. Bake at 375°F for ~45 minutes until tops are golden brown and internal bread temperature is 190–210°F. If bread gets too brown before it is done, cover with foil towards the end of the baking time.

Note: This is one of my favorite bread recipes. It is a true sourdough, no commercial yeast, but has some additional ingredients that improve flavor and rising times. Don't get impatient with this bread. It will seem like it is never going to rise, but then it does. Just give it time. Rising times are not as long as the Old Prospector's Sourdough Bread, but are still lengthy compared to regular bread. It has a good sourdough taste and keeps a little longer than the Old Prospector's Sourdough Bread does.

Improved Sourdough Bread

This bread will stay fresh longer than most loaves you'll make, due to both the olive oil and the sourdough starter; breads higher in acid retain moisture better than less acidic loaves.

To get one and a half (1½) or two (2) cups of starter to make your bread, take the one (1) cup of starter that you would normally put in the mixer's bowl and put it into a separate bowl. Feed this starter with ¾ cup warm water and 1 cup of Unbleached All-Purpose Flour. Stir until smooth, cover with plastic, and let it proof for 3-4 hours. Now you have one and a half (1½) or two (2) cups of starter ready to make your bread.

Ingredients

- *1 cup sourdough starter for a mildly sour taste.
- *1½ cups sourdough starter for a medium sour taste.
- *2 cups sourdough starter for a very sour taste.
- 1½ cups warm water
- 1 tablespoon active dry yeast or 2 teaspoons instant yeast
- 1 tablespoon salt
- ¼ cup olive oil
- 6 to 8 cups (approximately) Unbleached, All-Purpose Flour

Directions

1. In a large bowl, mix together the starter, water, and yeast. Add 3 cups of the flour.

2. Cover with plastic. Let this "sponge" sit overnight — up to 24 hours.

3. Place sponge into stand mixer bowl. Add the salt, oil, and about 2½ cups of flour. Knead until mixed and then add flour until the dough ball starts cleaning the sides of the bowl, around 5-10 minutes. This recipe uses two (2) cups of starter and will push the limits of a small stand mixer, so keep an eye on your dough as it kneads.

4. Turn the dough out onto a lightly floured or oiled work surface, and fold it several times.

5. Pour some olive oil into a bowl and use a paper towel to coat the sides of the bowl. Place the dough into the bowl and turn it to cover all sides with oil. Cover the bowl with plastic. Let it rise for 2 hours or until doubled in size.

6. Punch the dough down and divide it into two pieces. This recipe produces almost 1,500 grams of dough — just over three (3) pounds.

7. Knead each piece briefly on a lightly floured or oiled work surface. Form each piece into a round ball and place each ball on parchment or on a baking sheet that has been greased and

sprinkled with cornmeal. Cover the loaves with damp towels or lightly greased plastic wrap and allow them to rise for 1 hour (or more), or until they've just about doubled in size. (After this first loaf, you may want to put the dough into loaf pans to make "easier-to-use" sandwich bread.)

8. While the loaves are rising, preheat the oven to 375°F. Do this ahead of time so the oven is hot when you put the bread into the oven. Make three (3) slashes in the top of each loaf with a razor blade. (This helps the loaves to rise evenly in the oven). Bake the bread for 35 minutes or until it is golden brown and its interior measures 190°F to 205°F on an instant-read thermometer. Large loaves will take considerably longer to achieve the correct internal temperature. Remove the bread from the oven and cool completely on a wire rack.

Optional: Place a cast iron skillet in the bottom of the oven (on the bottom rack) before turning the oven on. When you put the bread into the oven to bake, toss a glass full of ice cubes into the skillet. This will steam the loaves during the first ten (10) minutes of baking, thus improving the crust. You can also place a shallow bowl on the bottom rack of the oven and put hot water into the bowl just before you turn on the oven.
Yield: 2–1½ pound loaves.

*You can adjust how sour your bread is — Mild, Medium, or Very Sour.

Comments: When you use one (1) cup of starter, this recipe makes a slightly less sour tasting bread than the other two (2) recipes. Even people who don't like sourdough bread usually enjoy this bread. Using one and a half (1½) or two (2) cups of starter makes a more sour bread. This bread is easy to make and has shorter rising times.

Congratulations!

You now have your first loaf of sourdough!

Chapter Six:
Some Technical Talk

How Does Sourdough Bread Work?

How do we make bread without adding commercial yeast? What makes our sourdough bread sour? How does all this work?

Sourdough bread derives from a centuries-old technology for preserving and storing yeast for long periods of time. People discovered that, by using this method of storing and preserving yeast, their bread produced amazing flavor.

When we purchase yeast today, we get yeast that has been meticulously cultured over decades to reproduce rapidly and to store well in a dry form. This is the commercial yeast of today.

But hundreds of years ago, people cultured yeast themselves and kept it alive using a medium called sourdough starter. This method of keeping yeast allows that particular yeast culture to last for years and years. In fact, some batches of starter have themselves been around for decades, passed from friend to friend or generation to generation.

So exactly what is going on in our yeast culture?

Yeast, Gluten, and Carbon Dioxide

You make sourdough bread from the same basic ingredients that you use for any other bread. The two most important ingredients are flour and yeast.

Yeast is a single-celled fungus that breaks down the starches in wheat flour, forming sugar. This process is called fermentation. When the yeast works on the starch and sugar molecules, it gives off carbon dioxide gas and alcohol. Yeast is a leavening agent for bread. It is what makes the bread rise.

Flour comes from any kind of ground grain, but most bread contains wheat flour. Two proteins found in wheat flour, gliadin and glutenin, form a stretchy substance called gluten. When you knead dough, you help gluten form long, threadlike chains. These gluten chains help hold the carbon dioxide gas in, creating those tiny holes that create the airy texture of bread.

The difference between sourdough bread and the "normal" bread you buy or bake today is the source of the yeast. Most bakers today use commercially cultivated yeast that comes in a package or jar. The package contains live yeast fungi in a state of hibernation. The yeast has been dried, preserved, and formed into a powder. You add flour, water, sugar, and salt to the yeast to make a loaf of bread. The water re-activates the yeast fungi, which feeds on the sugar and starch to make the bread rise.

Sourdough bread deals with yeast in a completely different way. Sourdough yeast fungi are actually kept alive constantly in a liquid medium called a starter. The baker either captures wild yeast that floats in the air and uses it to create starter from scratch, or gets a cup of active starter from a friend or purchases a starter and expands it.

Why Does Sourdough Bread Taste Sour?

The starter will also have a bacteria, lactobacilli, in it. This lends to the slightly acidic flavor of the bread by creating lactic acid! The alcohol that the yeast creates and the lactic acid together are the source of sourdough bread's unique flavor.

A common question at this point is, why doesn't our starter get infested with all kinds of other living organisms, such as mold and other bacteria? The answer is, sometimes it does. We have to be careful while handling our starter to protect it from getting contaminated. Try to keep your bowls, jars, and tools very clean while working with your starter. Some people have special bowls, jars, and tools that they use only for working with their starter. But this doesn't guarantee that your starter won't get contaminated. Just be careful, and watch for signs of contamination, such as an odd color and smell.

Our starter does a bit of self-preservation. Our starter also creates special enzymes to deal with starch and the starch in bread does not support a lot of other bacteria. The yeast and lactobacilli also "poison" the culture with the alcohol and lactic acid they produce, and that also keeps rogue bacteria under control.

Too high a build-up of the acid in our starter retards the yeast from happily doing their thing and imparts a stale taste to the bread. If this occurs, you can revitalize your starter by taking the jar of starter and dumping it out. Don't panic. Just pour out the starter leaving what stays in the jar on the sides and bottom. Put ¾ cup of warm (85-90°F) water in the jar and replace the top. Shake the jar to get all of that leftover starter mixed in the water. Pour this into a bowl and add one (1) cup of Unbleached All-Purpose Flour into the bowl and mix until smooth. Cover with plastic and let it proof until it is bubbly. Add another ¾ cup of warm water (85-90°F) and one (1) cup of flour to the starter. Mix until smooth. Cover with plastic and let sit until bubbly. After washing the jar thoroughly, pour this new starter in the jar and place it in the refrigerator. Your new starter should be fine getting a fresh start.

What Does "Primetime" for Starters Mean?

When your starter is working (proofing, fermenting), it will reach that stage we call "bubbly." Once your starter gets to that stage, it is considered to be at its "prime." This is the correct time to use it for making bread or to replace it into the jar to put back in the refrigerator, according to what you are doing at the time.

If you let your starter continue working beyond this "prime" time, it will start to go flat. If, for some reason, you forget that you have some starter working, just dump out the starter leaving ½ - 1 cup of starter in the bowl. Feed it (3/4 cup warm water and one (1) cup of flour) and let it work again.

Please take a quick look at the Troubleshooting chapter in this book if you have any problems. Also, reread the book and pay close attention to the details laid forth in the book.

Washing the Starter

If you have followed the instructions on maintaining your starter and made sure that all your cooking utensils have been thoroughly cleaned, you should not get a contaminated starter. If you have kept a back-up starter, you can just throw out the contaminated starter and just revive your back-up starter. But, if you have ended up with a contaminated starter and no back-up starter, you may be able to save the contaminated starter using the following method.

Take the contaminated started out of the refrigerator and allow it to get to room temperature (70–75°F). Pour out the starter, leaving just what sticks to the sides of the jar. Add ¾ cup of warm water (75–80°F) to the jar and replace the top. Shake the water in the jar until it removes all the starter left on the sides of the jar. Pour the water into a bowl and add 1 cup of unbleached flour. Mix until smooth. Cover the bowl with plastic and allow the bowl to set in a warm environment (~75°F).

Since you are starting with just a minimum of yeast, this ferment time will be long. Just keep an eye on the starter and when it starts to bubble remove the plastic and mix the starter. Add ¾ cup of warm water (70–75°F) and a cup of unbleached flour and mix until smooth. Place plastic over the bowl and allow this mixture to ferment. This time, it should take less time for the starter to get bubbly.

After several feedings of the starter, you should be back to a viable starter.

Chapter Seven:
Now What?

OK, you've created your first loaf of sourdough bread. What do you think? Is it as good as you expected it to be? Are you happy with your experience? I am confident that your first loaf turned out well, and that you love your sourdough bread. I would highly recommend that you create several more loaves of sourdough bread using these instructions and measurements. I do this for a couple of reasons.

1. If you have had some bad experiences with sourdough before this, duplicating your success will build your confidence that you can create great sourdough bread.

2. The more you go through the stages of taking your sourdough starter to the finished loaf, the better you will get at planning your time so your bread will finish when you want it to finish.

Once you have a couple of loaves of sourdough bread under your belt (no pun intended), you can try using your starter for sourdough pancakes or waffles. You will find recipes for these breakfast items in the next chapter.

The big thing to remember is that you must plan ahead for sourdough. You can't just get up one morning and say, "I think I'll make sourdough pancakes or waffles for breakfast." You need to plan for your sourdough breakfast items the evening before.

If sourdough is getting under your skin and you would like to try other types of yeast cultures, you can get yeast culture from hundreds of suppliers from around the world. You will find in the index of this book a list of sources for sourdough starters and other books on sourdough. Two (2) of these books I highly recommend to anyone interested in taking their sourdough baking to the next level.

The first one is "Classic Sourdoughs" by Ed Wood and Jean Wood, the revised edition. This is exactly what the subtitle states, "A Home Baker's Handbook." This book was originally published in 1996. Jean has since passed away, but she and Ed have created a legacy for sourdough bakers everywhere.

The second book is only for those who really want to gear up their sourdough (or any bread) baking to a professional or commercial level. Its title is, "Bread: A Baker's Book of Techniques and Recipes." The author is Jeffrey Hamelman. Mr. Hamelman is the Director of the Bakery and Bakery Education Center at King Arthur Flour Company in Vermont. This is a very technical book geared more to the commercial bakery business than the home baker, but his recipes do have a home baker proportions column. The insight you can gain from reading either or both of these books is invaluable.

In Part II of this book, I provide insight into what makes sourdough work and what you can do to make better sourdough. It will help you troubleshoot any problems you run into while baking your sourdough.

The recipe section of Part II contains some more advanced sourdough recipes for you to try. It will also contain some recipes for bread that, while not technically being sourdough, use the same methodology used to make sourdough. Breads like French and Ciabatta breads use a "starter," also called a "sponge," to create the unique characteristics of those breads.

Chapter Eight:
Recipes

This section contains several additional recipes for you to try. Until you gain some knowledge and experience with baking, I would stick to the recipes fairly closely. Once you have some experience baking, and especially baking sourdough, you can try whatever you would like.

One rule of thumb with sourdough — rising times always take longer than you think they will. Don't paint yourself into a corner time-wise.

The recipes included in this section are:

Old Prospector's Classic Sourdough Bread.
This is the same recipe we practiced with above. It's a basic, pure sourdough. This recipe includes ingredients for small, medium, large, and extra-large loaves. (Long Rising Times)

Sourdough Pancakes
This is a great recipe to use the half (one cup) of starter that you discard when feeding your starter.

Sourdough Waffles
For those who prefer waffles to pancakes.

Sourdough Ciabatta Bread
Ciabatta bread is different from other breads. The dough doesn't look or act like regular bread dough. It

is VERY sticky — as if it doesn't have enough flour in it. Do Not Be Tempted to add more flour. That is the way the dough is supposed to be.

Regular Ciabatta Bread
When you prefer a non-sourdough Ciabatta Bread.

Crusty French Bread
This is an easy and much quicker bread to make. It is not sourdough, but it makes a wonderful complement to pasta.

Sourdough Biscuits
A breakfast favorite.

Sourdough Baguettes
Another bread favorite.

Sourdough Garlic Breadsticks
Another pasta favorite.

Sourdough Pizza Crust
Better than the local pizza place.

Old Prospector's Classic Sourdough Bread

Ingredients for Small Loaf

- 1 cup starter
- 1 cup water – 240 ml
- 1 teaspoon salt
- 3½ cups Unbleached All-Purpose Flour – 490 g

Ingredients for Medium Loaf

- 1¼ cup starter
- 1¼ cup water – 300 g
- 1¼ teaspoons salt
- 4 3/8 cup Unbleached All-Purpose Flour – 613 g

Ingredients for Large Loaf

- 1½ cup starter
- 1½ cup water – 360 g
- 1½ teaspoons salt
- 5¼ cups Unbleached All-Purpose Flour – 735 g

Ingredients for Extra Large Loaf

- 2 cups starter
- 2 cups water – 480 g
- 2 teaspoons salt
- 7 cups Unbleached All-Purpose Flour – 980 g

Note: To get one and a half (1½) or two (2) cups of starter to make your bread, take the one (1) cup of starter that you would normally put in the mixer's bowl and put it into a separate bowl. Feed this starter with ¾ cup warm water and 1 cup of Unbleached All-Purpose Flour. Stir until smooth, cover with plastic, and let it proof for 3-4 hours. Now you have one and a half (1½) or two (2) cups of starter ready to make your bread.

Directions

1. Put the starter in the bowl. Add water and salt to the starter. Mix. Add flour, 1 cup at a time, until dough is too stiff to mix by hand. Turn onto a floured board and knead in remaining flour until dough is smooth and satiny. Or, mix and knead all ingredients in mixer no longer than 25 minutes. (*Caution!* If you are making a large or extra-large loaf, the dough will climb up the dough hook and try to invade the planetary drive of your mixer. You will need to stop kneading often and push the dough down.)

2. Place in an oiled (olive oil) bowl, flip so all sides are coated with oil, and cover with plastic.

3. Proof overnight (8–12 hours). Dough should double in size. Turn onto a floured board.

4. Cover and allow to rest for 30 minutes. If marked flattening occurs, knead in additional flour before shaping.

5. After 30 minute's rest, shape dough. Shaping is important as any creases left in the dough will become canyons in your finished loaf. Put any creases left on the dough on the bottom of the loaf.

6. Place loaf on baking sheet that has been greased or on parchment paper, or in a Dutch oven, or in the appropriate size sauce pan. Cover with plastic and let rise either at room temperature or a little warmer (75-80°F) for 2-4 hours or until doubled in size.

Note: Proofing at higher temperatures (90°F) equals a more sour loaf with good taste, but decreased leavening. Proofing at room temperature will yield good leavening and mild sourness. Proofing at room temperature for the first hour, and then at 90°F until risen will yield a moderately sour loaf with only slightly decreased leavening.

7. Slash top of loaf with a razor blade. Spray with water (preferred), or gently brush with olive oil. Place loaf into a COOL oven, then turn the temperature to 375°F and bake for 70 minutes. OR, place loaf on preheated baking stone in a 450°F oven and bake for 40 minutes.

First Baking Method vs. Second Baking Method Tips:

From Number 7 above, if you are using the first baking method (putting the bread into a cool oven), spray water into the oven at 5 minute intervals after the oven reaches 212°F. Do this three (3) times. Have shallow bowl of water in bottom of oven. If you are baking your sourdough loaf in a covered Dutch oven or sauce pan, there is no need to spray water in the oven or have a shallow bowl of water in bottom of oven.

If you are using the second method of baking (putting dough into a hot oven), spray oven with water every 5 minutes for 15 minutes. Place a shallow oven-proof bowl of water on the bottom rack of the oven. If you are baking your sourdough loaf in a covered Dutch oven or sauce pan, there is no need to spray water in the oven or have a shallow bowl of water in bottom of oven.

Sourdough Pancakes

Ingredients

- ¾ cup sourdough starter
- 1 egg, beaten
- 2 tablespoons water
- 2 teaspoons vegetable oil
- 1/3 cup non-fat dry milk powder
- ¾ teaspoon salt
- 1 teaspoon baking soda
- 1½ tablespoons white sugar

Directions

1. In a large bowl, combine the sourdough starter, egg, water, and oil.

2. In a separate bowl, combine the non-fat dry milk, salt, baking soda, and sugar. Stir to blend dry ingredients. Add to sourdough starter and mix until batter is smooth.

3. Bake on a greased 350 degree F (175 degree C) griddle until golden brown on the bottom. Flip and bake on opposite side.

Sourdough Waffles

To get two (2) cups of starter to make your bread, take the one (1) cup of starter that you would normally put in the mixer's bowl and put it into a separate bowl. Feed this starter with ¾ cup warm water and 1 cup of Unbleached All-Purpose Flour. Stir until smooth, cover with plastic, and let it proof for 3-4 hours. Now you have two (2) cups of starter ready to make your waffles.

Ingredients

- 2 cups starter
- 2 Tablespoons sugar
- 4 Tablespoons oil
- 1 egg
- ½ teaspoon salt
- 1 teaspoon baking soda
- ¼ cup warm water

Directions

1. Put starter in a large bowl, add sugar, egg, oil, and salt mixing well.

2. Dilute the soda in the warm water and fold gently into batter. Do not beat

3. Gently stir until dough doubles in size. Ladle some batter into a pre-heated waffle iron. When the waffle iron stops steaming, the waffle is ready.

Sourdough Ciabatta (Italian Bread)

Ingredients:

- 1 cup sourdough starter, room temperature
- ¾ cup warm water (80-90°F)
- 2 tablespoons extra-virgin olive oil
- 1½ teaspoons salt
- 1 tablespoon granulated sugar
- 1½ cups bread flour
- ½ cup white whole wheat flour
- 1 teaspoon instant yeast

This bread dough will end up being a very sticky, wet dough. Do not add any additional flour to the dough.

Directions:

1. Place all ingredients into your mixer's bowl. Mix on speed 1 at first and then on speed 2. Mix until dough is mixed well. It will look more like batter than bread dough.

2. Mix until dough is mixed well. It will look more like batter than bread dough.

3. Remove dough from pan and place into a large, oiled bowl. Cover with plastic wrap and let rise at room temperature approximately 1½ hours or until tripled in bulk (dough will be sticky and full of bubbles).

4. On a baking sheet, place a sheet of parchment paper. Sprinkle parchment paper lightly with flour. Turn the risen dough onto a flour dusted work surface. Pat dough (do not punch down) into a rectangle and dust with flour. Transfer to prepared baking sheet. Press fingertips into dough in several places to dimple surface. Cover dough with plastic wrap and let rise at room temperature for 1½ to 2 hours or until doubled in size.

5. At least 45 minutes before baking, place baking stones on lowest oven rack in oven and set the temperature to 500°F. Allow the oven to heat for 30 minutes.

6. Lower oven temperature to 400°F. Transfer loaf (with parchment paper) to the hot baking stones. Bake 15 minutes or until pale golden. A good check is to use an instant digital thermometer to test your bread. The temperature should be between 200 and 210°F.

7. Remove from oven and place the bread on a wire rack to cool. Let baked loaf cool for 30 minutes before cutting (this is because the bread is still cooking while it is cooling).

Makes 1 large loaf.

Regular Ciabatta Bread (Italian Bread)

Ingredients

- 4 cups flour – 3½ white and ½ white whole wheat
- ¼ teaspoon yeast
- 1½ teaspoons salt
- 2 cups warm water

Directions

1. Mix all ingredients. Dough will be very sticky. Cover with plastic wrap. Let rise 18 hours.

2. Punch down with spatula.

3. Place parchment on sheet pan or baking stone. Here's a trick. Spray work surface with water. Put plastic sheet onto sprayed work surface.

4. Sprinkle plastic sheet with flour. Put dough on surface. Sprinkle with flour.

5. Pull/stretch into long, flat loaf. Flip loaf off plastic onto pan.

6. Sprinkle lightly with flour. Cover with plastic. Let rise for 2 hours.

7. Bake at 425°F for 35–45 minutes.

Crusty French Bread

Ingredients

- 1 (.25 ounce) package active dry yeast
- 1 cup warm water (80°F -90°F)
- 2 tablespoons sugar
- 2 tablespoons olive oil
- 1½ teaspoons salt
- 3 cups all-purpose flour
- 1 egg white
- 1 teaspoon cold water

Directions

1. In a large mixing bowl, dissolve yeast in warm water. Add the sugar, oil, salt, and 2 cups flour. Beat until blended. Stir in enough remaining flour to form a stiff dough.

2. Turn onto a floured surface; knead until smooth and elastic, about 6-8 minutes. Place in a greased bowl, turning once to grease top. Cover and let rise in a warm place until doubled, about 1 hour. Punch dough down; return to bowl. Cover and let rise for 30 minutes.

3. Punch dough down. Turn onto a lightly floured surface. Shape into a loaf 16 in. long x 2½ in. wide with tapered ends. Sprinkle a greased baking sheet with cornmeal; place loaf

on baking sheet. Cover and let rise until doubled, about 25 minutes.

4. Beat egg white and cold water; brush over dough. With a sharp knife, make diagonal slashes 2 in. apart across top of loaf. Bake at 375°F for 25-30 minutes or until golden brown. Remove from pan to a wire rack to cool.

Sourdough Biscuits

Ingredients

- 2 cups all-purpose flour
- 1 tablespoon sugar
- 1 tablespoon baking powder
- ¾ teaspoon salt
- 2 cups sourdough starter
- 2 to 3 tablespoons softened butter

Directions

1. Mix flour, sugar, baking powder, and salt into a large bowl; pour in starter.

2. Mix to make a firm dough.

3. Place parchment on baking sheet. Pinch off walnut-sized balls and place on pan. Or you can roll-out the dough to around ¾ inch thick and use a biscuit cutter to cut out the biscuits.

4. Let stand in a warm place 10 to 15 minutes.

5. Bake in 400°F oven for 24 to 30 minutes.

Sourdough Baguettes

Ingredients

- 1¼ cups lukewarm water
- 2 cups sourdough starter, about the consistency of thick pancake batter; fed, or unfed*
- 4½ to 5 cups Unbleached All-Purpose Flour
- 2½ teaspoons salt
- 2 teaspoons sugar
- 1 tablespoon instant yeast
- 4 teaspoons <u>vital wheat gluten</u> — if you have it**
- 1 egg yolk lightly beaten with 1 tablespoon water, for glaze; optional

*If you feed your sourdough before using, the loaves will rise better; but if you're in a hurry, unfed sourdough will simply lend its flavor, while the yeast in the recipe takes care of the rise.

** Diastatic malt contains active enzymes which help break starch down into sugar. The extra sugar feeds the yeast in the dough, helping the bread to rise, and also gives the bread a browner crust. Don't worry if you don't have it.

Tips: Want to make just 3 baguettes instead of 6? Or two short, fat Italian-style loaves? Cut all of the ingredients except the yeast in half, leaving the yeast at 1 tablespoon.

Directions

1. In a large bowl, combine the water, starter, and 3 cups of the flour, mixing until smooth.

2. Stir in the salt, sugar, yeast, and gluten, then an additional 1½ to 2 cups of flour. Stir until the dough pulls away from the sides of the bowl, adding only enough additional flour as necessary; a slack (sticky) dough makes a light loaf.

3. Knead the dough for about 7 minutes in a stand mixer; or 8 to 10 minutes by hand, on a lightly greased work surface. You may also knead this dough using the dough cycle on your bread machine; once it's finished kneading, transfer it to a bowl to rise, as directed below.

4. Turn the dough into an oiled bowl, cover the bowl, and let the dough rise until doubled in size, about 90 minutes.

5. Gently deflate the dough, and divide it into six pieces (for thin baguettes) or three pieces (for thicker Italian loaves).

6. Shape each piece into a 16" long loaf and place the loaves, at least 4" apart, on parchment-lined baking sheets or in lightly greased baguette pans (French loaf pans). If you're using baguette pans, make the loaves 15" long.

7. Cover the loaves with lightly greased plastic wrap and let them rise for 1½ to 2 hours or until they're nice and puffy. Towards the end of the rising time, preheat your oven to 450°F.

8. If desired, gently brush the loaves with egg yolk glaze and sprinkle them generously with Pizza Seasoning, artisan bread topping, or the toppings of your choice. If you're not brushing the loaves with egg yolk, spray them with olive oil spray; this will help them brown.

9. For a classic look, make three diagonal slashes in each loaf, cutting about ¼ in. deep. For taller, rounder baguettes, don't slash.

10. Bake the baguettes for about 25 minutes or until they're a rich golden brown. Remove the loaves from the oven. Turn off the oven, crack it open a few inches, and return the loaves to the cooling oven without their pans. Letting the loaves cool right in the turned-off oven helps preserve their crunchy crust.

Yield: 6 baguettes or 3 Italian-style loaves.

Sourdough Garlic Breadsticks

Ingredients

For the sponge
- 1/3 cup starter
- 1 cup bread flour
- ¾ cup milk
- Mix well

Dough
- 4 cups bread flour (about)
- 1 cup milk
- 1 Tablespoon Italian seasoning
- 1 Tablespoon minced garlic (fresh or wet ready to use)
- 1 cup shredded cheddar cheese
- ¼ cup soft butter
- 1¼ teaspoons salt

Coating
- 1 cube melted butter
- Sea salt
- Garlic powder

Directions

1. Mix ingredients for sponge, cover, and put in a warm draft free place. When sponge is developed, mix the dough ingredients in a stand mixer bowl with flat blade.
2. Change to dough hook, add sponge and run dough hook about six minutes. Stop as needed

to remove dough from hook if dough is just going round and round. Varying speed can also help prevent sliding. Add flour or water as needed to achieve slightly stiff dough.

3. Place on floured board and knead for several minutes until pliable. Roll into a rectangle, about six inches wide and 5/8 inches thick. With a sharp knife cut strips about 6″ X 5/8″ X 5/8″. There should be about twenty pieces. On a board, roll these by hand into cylinders about nine inches long. Place on greased cookie sheet or jelly roll pan with about one inch between each stick.

4. Cover and let rise until double in size. Brush with melted butter and sprinkle with sea salt. Place in preheated 400°F oven and bake for about 12 minutes or until light brown. Remove and brush again with butter and sprinkle again with salt, then with garlic powder. Allow to cool before serving.

Sourdough Pizza Crust

Ingredients

- 1½ cups sourdough starter
- 1 Tablespoon olive oil
- 1 teaspoon salt
- 1½ cups flour

Directions

1. Preheat oven to 450°F.

2. Mix ingredients, working in the flour until you have a soft dough. If the dough gets too dry, add some more starter or add a little water.

3. Once you've kneaded the dough, cover it and let rest for ½ hour. This lets the dough relax, so forming the pizza is easier.

4. Once the dough has rested, roll the dough out into the shape you prefer — the traditional round (around 12 inches in diameter) or a rectangle (around 9 X 12 inches). Also, the crust thickness comes into play here.

5. Once you have your dough in the shape you want, you may pre-bake it or top it and bake it. To pre-bake it, slide the pie onto a baker's peel and then into the oven onto a baking stone. Bake about 5 minutes. It doesn't take long, so watch carefully.

5. Once the shell is pre-baked, you may cool it and then freeze it, or top it and finish baking it.

7. When you're ready to top the pizza, rub a bit of olive oil on the surface, as this helps keep the crust from getting soggy. Then top with your ingredients.

8. Whatever your favorite topping, you want to balance the cooking time so the crust is nicely browned and the cheese topping has browned a bit. It is a kind of an adventure—anywhere from 15 to 25 minutes, depending on the temperature and toppings, should work.

Chapter Nine:
Troubleshooting—
What am I doing wrong?

My bread rises, but it does so horizontally, resulting in a very flat loaf. Other than this, the bread is tasty.

You need to add some more flour to your dough. Remember, if you are using a stand mixer, the dough ball should clean all the flour residue off the sides and bottom of the mixer's bowl.

It's been 12 hours and bread dough is still not rising.

If the starter was bubbly when you made the dough, give it more time. If you use less starter, you will actually wind up with a more sour flavor, but it might take 24 hours to get to the first rise. When it doubles in size, punch it down and let it rise again.

My bread rises, but then it falls during baking.

You have left out the salt or have not added enough of it. Salt actually retards rising slightly, but strengthens the gluten so the loaf will keep its shape. Use at least 1 teaspoon of salt for every 3 cups of flour.

<u>My bread just doesn't bake right. It turns brown and gets a crust before it rises in the oven. It just doesn't look like a store-bought loaf.</u>

Several things can cause this. Make sure you catch your sponge at its peak (prime), which will help to rise the bread more. Your starter has become too acidic; dump most of it out and start over using a few tablespoons of the old starter. Too much butter — don't use any at all next time to see if this is the problem.

<u>My bread is not chewy enough.</u>

Add some butter, or use a second or even a third rise.

<u>My bread is not crispy enough.</u>

Use less butter and/or reduce the kneading time. When the loaf comes out of the oven, you should hear and see the crust start to crack. This is a good indication of a good crispy crust with the right amount of water and kneading. To save the existing loaf, keep it in the oven as the oven is cooling down to dry out the crust some more.

<u>I slash the top of the bread, but my knife tears and stretches the loaf.</u>

Use a very sharp knife. Spray cooking oil on the knife blade. Some people have good success using a wet razor blade (in France, this is mounted to a holder and called a Lame, pronounced lam). Also, try spraying the loaf with water. But be careful; too much water will flatten out the loaf. I also just dip my razor blade in some flour for each slash.

<u>After rising, my loaf just became flat, looks a little wet, and has a very strong, sour smell.</u>

Too much acid/alcohol in the starter. You need to dump out most of the starter. You can try to revive your starter by dumping all of it out, preserving only the small amount that sticks to the sides of the jar. Add an equal amount of flour and water and let it set and rebuild itself.

<u>My bread is not sour enough.</u>

The sour taste is usually a function of time. The longer you let the bread rise, the more sour the taste. If the yeast culture is very active and you simply can't let it rise any longer, use two or three rises, punching down the loaf in between. You can also add a few tablespoons of white rye flour, which will enhance the sourdough flavor. If you are using any commercial yeast in your recipe, try adding a bit more starter in the beginning.

<u>My bread doesn't brown properly or is not very crispy.</u>

Not enough steam during baking. Fill a spray bottle with water and spray the inside of the stoneware bowl and top of the loaf before baking. Too much butter—don't use butter at all or cut back half of what you're using. Also try adding a couple of tablespoons of sugar in the recipe.

<u>I've tried everything, and I still can't get the dough to rise enough.</u>

Add some malted barley flour when mixing the dough, about 1-2 teaspoons (5-10ml) per 3 cups of flour. Some people add Diastatic Malt powder or Ascorbic Acid (Vitamin C crystals) which will increase and speed up the rise considerably. These additives can change the color, texture, and flavor of your bread, so precede cautiously.

If all else fails, go back to the basics. If you have made bread successfully, go back to a recipe and use the same rising conditions you did with that bread. Make sure you can still make a good loaf of bread. When we start experimenting with recipes and techniques, we can expect some "less-than-successful" results. Don't get discouraged. Just go back to the basics and try again.

In Part II, I go into more detail of the technical aspects of making sourdough bread. Like I said before, it's not rocket science, unless you want it to be. Approaching making sourdough bread on a commercial basis is an entire different universe. Be sure to read Jeffrey Hamelman's book, "Bread — A Baker's Book of Techniques and Recipes" if this is your intent.

PART II

Moving Beyond the Basics

Introduction

This part of the book contains more advanced information on sourdough baking. This information can help you to make better sourdough bread with more consistent results.

Sourdough baking is susceptible to many factors. Most of you would be quick to say that temperature is a major factor. This is true, but temperature is even more complicated than just keeping the rising area around a certain temperature. Professional bakers have a desired "dough temperature" in mind when they begin mixing their bread ingredients. They measure the flour temperature and then calculate the needed water temperature to get the dough temperature results they desire. While we, as home bakers, don't need to make hundreds of loaves of bread a day, an understanding of dough temperature can help us make consistently superb sourdough bread.

Proofing temperatures are important, as well. In this book, you will find instructions on constructing a "Proofing Box." A proofing box is where you will put your starter to ferment and your bread dough to rise. You will be able to control the temperature in your proofing box so your starter/bread will proof at the optimum temperature. It will also allow you to change your proofing temperature during the proof to meet some of the more complex sourdough bread recipes' demands. The building instructions for the

Proofing Box is simple and shouldn't cost more than $25-$30 in supplies.

Another investment I am going to ask you to make is an accurate digital scale—one that weighs in both ounces and grams. A scale will change your baking life forever. It allows you to be very accurate and consistent in your ingredient measurements, thus resulting in better bread. For example, I can have three (3) people measure out one (1) cup of flour and if we weigh all three measures they will most likely be different. Weight is constant—volume, with the human factor thrown in, is not.

If you do not have a stand mixer with a dough hook, you may want to consider getting one. I know they are expensive, but a good stand mixer with a dough hook will make your sourdough baking experience a lot easier and more fun.

It would be a good idea to get an oven thermometer just to make sure your oven is doing what it says it is doing.

So, let's get started. Some of the things I will talk about may be too technical for some. Don't worry about it. That information is there for those who want to really get an insight into sourdough baking.

Chapter 10:
Intermediate Basics

Though in Part I, I covered the basics of making sourdough bread, there are still "basics" for us to understand, even in this more advanced portion of the book.

We are going to discuss the process of making sourdough bread from mixing to baking. According to the recipe you are following and how complex you want to make the process, there can be many steps in the process. For the Master Baker, there are twelve (12) steps: Step 1 is Scaling (Measuring), Step 2 is Mixing, Step 3 is Bulk (Primary) Fermentation, Step 4 is Folding, Step 5 is Dividing, Step 6 is Pre-Shaping, Step 7 is Bench Rest, Step 8 is Shaping, Step 9 is Final Fermentation, Step 10 is Scoring, Step 11 is Baking, and Step 12 is Cooling. These steps are all important, especially to the commercial baker. For us home bakers, we can simplify the process a bit by combining some of the individual steps into a major step or two. The results are these five steps:

1. Measuring

2. Mixing

3. Primary Fermentation — which includes Folding, Dividing, Pre-Shaping & Bench Rest

4. Final Fermentation — which includes Shaping
    & Scoring

5. Baking — which includes Cooling.

We are going to cover these five steps in some
detail. You can determine how important each step is
to your bread making.

Measuring

A very important part of the bread-making
process is the accurate measurement of the
ingredients. We are so used to grabbing measuring
cups and spoons to portion our ingredients for the
recipe we are making. Some measurements are more
critical than others. Measuring two (2) tablespoons of
sugar can be adequately accomplished with a one (1)
tablespoon measuring spoon. But the flour and water

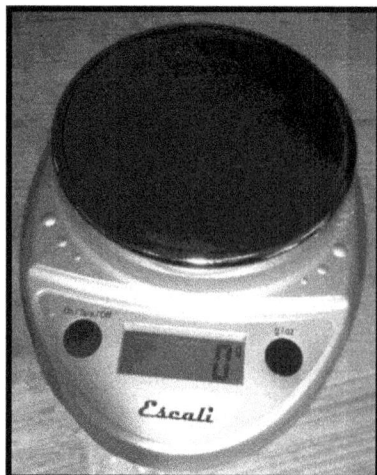

measurements are more critical and these measurements should be accomplished by weight, not volume. In the back of this book, is the Volume-to-Weight Conversion Chart (Index One) of the most common ingredients used in the kitchen. This chart is a guideline when measuring these ingredients. The only safe way to measure is to weigh each item as you use it. To do this, you should invest in an accurate scale.

Mixing

Most people think of mixing as just the uniform distribution of ingredients so that they are evenly dispersed in the bread dough. While this is true, a lot more happens when the ingredients are mixed. As soon as the water touches the flour in the mixing process, gluten starts being formed. The formation of gluten is necessary to strengthen the dough and allows the dough to hold the carbon dioxide (CO_2) produced by the fermenting yeast, thus making the bread rise. But this process is even more complicated than that. There are actually two (2) proteins in flour which combine to form the gluten — glutenin and gliadin. Each of these proteins have their own characteristics; glutenin helps the dough develop structure and elasticity, while gliadin provides the dough with the ability to be stretched. While these two (2) characteristics appear to be opposites, they need to work together, in balance, throughout the entire bread-production process. This may seem like useless information until you realize, for example, that rye flour contains gliadin, but very little glutenin and therefore requires different mixing techniques.

Mixing also introduces air, thus oxygen, into the bread dough or starter. When I feed my sourdough starter, I try to mix the added flour and water into the existing starter with some vigor. This helps aerate the starter and helps give the yeast a kick-start.

Autolyse: What the heck is autolyse? Autolyse is a technique developed by Professor Raymond Calvel, an expert on French Bread production. Basically, this technique mixes just the flour and water in a recipe at a very low speed—no salt, yeast, or pre-ferments. Once the flour and water are mixed, the dough is covered and left to rest for twenty (20) minutes to one (1) hour. As the flour fully hydrates, the gluten bonds despite of the lack of kneading. Once autolyse has completed, the balance of the mixing time is reduced. This is especially helpful with sourdough bread production. I also believe that an offshoot of the autolyse technique is the influx of "No-Knead" bread recipes that have flooded the industry in the last decade or two.

Mixing and kneading times are also important. One common mistake home bakers make is over-mixing and over-kneading. We want the dough to develop but not over-develop. Over-developed bread dough results in loss of color and taste. When using a typical home stand mixer with a dough hook, ballpark times are 2-2½ minutes on speed #1 to mix and 4-5 minutes on speed #2 to knead.

Other ingredients in the bread dough can hinder dough development. The lipids in fats, such as butter, oil, and eggs coat the gluten strands and delay their development. As the amount of fat in a recipe increases, the mixing time must also be longer. If there is a large amount of fat in the recipe, consider mixing the dough without the fats introduced and add them after the dough has been mixed.

Primary Fermentation

As soon as you turn off the mixer, dough fermentation begins. The oxygen mixed into the dough is rapidly consumed by the yeast and the fermentation begins in the absence of oxygen. Fermentation is the process of yeast consuming sugar and creating CO_2 and alcohol. This yeast came from either the wild yeast of a sourdough yeast culture, commercial yeast, or a combination of both. When I was brewing beer, I learned a lot about yeast. There is quite a difference between ale yeast, lager yeast, and wine yeast. Each of these categories contains many yeast strains as well. For brewing, the major differences are fermenting temperatures and the resistance to alcohol. Ale yeast ferments quite happily at 78-80°F. Lager yeast, on the other hand, does its finest work at 34°F. Beer yeast will die when the alcohol percentage gets to around 7%, while wine yeast can go strong to about 18%.

Bread yeast can function at temperatures between around freezing and around 130°F. The optimal range for wheat breads is 75-78°F and, for rye breads, it's around 80-83°F. Temperatures above 80°F will speed the fermentation process, but CO_2 development is not the only factor we are interested in during fermentation. Flavor can be sacrificed at higher fermentation temperatures, so the 75-78°F gives us a good balance between volume and flavor.

There are four (4) other steps that we have included in the Primary Fermentation step. "Folding" may seem like a minor step. But proper folding can make quite a difference in your bread. Many recipes call for "punching" down your dough a time or two during the primary fermentation. But proper folding will have better results.

Folding

So why do we "punch" down or fold the dough? Many people think that it is just to "degas" the dough. True, we want to accomplish this process, but there is more to it than just degassing. First, let's talk about how to properly fold your dough.

Flour your work surface with enough flour to keep the dough from sticking to the work area. Place the dough onto the floured surface and turn it so both sides have a lightly floured surface. We don't want to incorporate additional flour into the dough so, if we get too much flour on the dough surface, we must brush off the excess flour with each fold we make.

Start with either the left side or the right side—your choice. Let's say we start with the left side in this example. Take the left side of the dough and lift about 1/3 of the dough up and over the rest of the dough. Make sure there is no excess flour on the dough as you fold it. If there is excess flour, brush it off with your hand before it gets incorporated into the dough. Once you have that 1/3 of the dough folded over onto the dough, gently press down on the dough to force the captured gas out. Don't overdo this.

Now take the opposite side of the dough—in this case, the right side—and lift the right 1/3 of the dough and fold it over on top of the previously folded dough. Again, gently press down on the dough to force the captured gas out.

Now repeat the process using the top and bottom 1/3 of the dough. This is the proper method of folding the dough.

How many times should I fold the dough during the Primary Fermentation? This will vary between dough types and recipes. Generally, dough that requires 1½ hours or more in Primary Fermentation should be folded at least once during the rise to degas the dough. Dough that is made from "weak" flour benefits from extra folds. Dough that is highly "hydrated," such as Ciabatta dough, benefits from extra folds. I won't go into detail on hydration in this book—if you want to know more about hydration, I highly recommend Jeffery Hamelman's book, <u>Bread – A Baker's Book of Techniques and Recipes.</u> But if you have made Ciabatta before, you know enough to understand the basics of hydration, as Ciabatta bread dough always seems to have way too much water in the dough.

Dividing

Technically, the Primary Fermentation ends when (if) the dough is divided. As home bakers, the dough we are mixing often makes just one loaf of bread. If that is the case, then we do not need to divide the dough. But there are times we do need to divide the dough to make two (2) or three (3) loaves from our dough. A metal dough cutter (I use my general kneading board scraper — see photo), and a good scale is all that is needed to properly divide the dough.

Form the dough into a shape that allows you to easily "eyeball" the center of the dough for dividing the dough into two (2) parts, or 1/3 of the dough, if you are making three (3) loaves. If you are making four (4) loaves, first divide the dough in half, then divide each half in half. Cut the dough with the dough cutter and weigh the divided dough segments.

Try to get each portion of dough the same weight. If you need to pinch off a small amount from a heavier portion and add it to a smaller portion, do so. The idea is to get each portion as close to the same weight as possible. This will simplify rising and baking.

Pre-Shaping

Once the dough is divided (if you needed to divide the dough), we want to pre-shape the dough into closely the same shape we want the final shape to be. I prefer to place any seams down during the pre-shape process. Some bakers don't care which side of the dough is up or down, but I believe the dough will rise more uniformly when the seams are placed underneath.

Bench-Rest

The Bench-Rest is a period of time to allow the dough to relax. Cover your pre-shaped dough with plastic so it doesn't form a dry crust during the Bench-Rest. This Rest period isn't set in concrete—just allow the dough to relax 20-30 minutes before performing the Shaping process.

Final Fermentation

Final Fermentation occurs after the dough is shaped and before it is loaded into the oven to bake.

With experience, you will get to know just how much the dough *can* rise in a particular time period. You mustn't let the dough over-rise. Ideally, the dough should be placed into the oven when it has risen to 85-90% of its finished size. We usually will say, "let the dough rise until it has doubled in size." This is a good statement, but it is sometimes difficult to determine exactly when the dough has "doubled" in size. Some breads, such as Ciabatta, will rise horizontally more than vertically. Pay attention to your bread in this Final Fermentation—even take notes as to time and size—so you will gain the working knowledge you need to make the best bread possible.

Shaping

After the Bench-Rest, the dough is Shaped into the shape it needs to be for Final Fermentation (rising). This could be a round shape, an oblong shape, long narrow shape, or a shape to fit into a baking pan. Once shaped, cover with plastic to avoid it drying out, and place it in your "rising area." If it will fit into your proofing box, great. If not, or you do not have a proofing box, the area you used for your Primary Fermentation will suffice.

Scoring

When the dough reaches the end of its Final Fermentation, it is ready to be scored and baked.

Some breads, such as the braided breads, Ciabattas, and most bread baked in a traditional bread pan, are not scored. Your typical sourdough loaf is almost always scored. Scoring is not just for looks. The score(s) in the top of the loaf allows the bread to expand during the first few minutes of baking (often called Oven Spring) under control. If you do not score the loaf, the bread will have difficulty expanding evenly and will most often break on the surface's weakest point.

There are no rules to scoring and there are as many different ways to score bread as there are bakers. On round loaves, I have scored three (3) parallel cuts, four (4) cuts in the shape of a Tic-Tack-Toe game, and just one (1) long score. On oblong loaves, I like to score the loaf with cuts on a 45 degree angle to the length of the loaf approximately 2 inches (51mm) apart. I try to score my typical loaf of bread to around 3/8 to ½ inch deep. The beginning baker will usually err to scoring too shallow and the score(s) will almost disappear during the baking. Scoring is best accomplished by using a razor blade that you dip in flour just before each cut. If you do not dip your razor blade into flour before each cut, the blade will drag in the dough and deform your beautiful loaf.

Baking

We have gone through a lot of processes to get to this point, but Baking is where we reap the fruits of our labors. In the Baking process, there is a lot more going on than you probably want to know. I will not go into all the details (again, if you wish to investigate this in more detail, refer to Jeffery Hamelman's book), but I will outline the major components of the Baking process.

During the first few minutes of the Baking process, something very obvious occurs to the bread; it completes its last bit of rising (fermentation) in a very short period of time. This is called Oven Spring. There are a couple of reasons for this phenomenon: first, the sudden increase in the ambient temperature causes the yeast to accelerate its last effort of fermentation. This is accompanied by the production of CO_2 gas, thus causing a rapid-rising effect. Second, the trapped CO_2 gas in the dough expands which adds to this rapid rise.

As the dough temperature approaches 140°F (60°C), all yeast and bacteria die. From around 140° to 160°F (60°–70°C), the wheat starch begins to gelatinize and the coagulation of gluten begins. From around 160° to 175°F (70°–80°C), gluten coagulation is complete and the dough structure is formed. From around 175° to 195°F (80º–90°C), the wheat starch gelatinization is complete. From around 195° to 212°F (90°–100°C), maximum internal loaf temperature is reached and crust coloration begins. From around 212° to 350°F (100°–177°C), crust color deepens and several chemical reactions occur that contribute to flavor and aroma. From around 300°F to 400°F (150°–204°C), further crust color and flavor development occurs through the caramelization process.

Like I said earlier, this is probably more information than you need or want to know, but there it is for your enjoyment. It is important to know that the crust of the bread is the only part of the bread where the temperature exceeds 212°F (100°C). I will usually use my digital thermometer to measure the internal temperature of my bread toward the end of the baking period. The target I am aiming for is an internal temperature of between 195° and 205°F (90°-95° C).

Moisture Content in Bread

Let's talk a little about moisture in bread — in the finished loaf and during the baking process. A baked loaf of bread will always weigh less than it did before it was baked. Water in the dough evaporates during the baking process — from 10-20% is normal. There are several factors that affect the moisture loss in baked bread:

- Loaf Weight: A larger loaf of bread will tend to lose less moisture.

- Loaf Shape: A long, skinny loaf of bread, such as baguettes (which have a high crust to crumb ratio [crumb is the inner part of the bread]) lose a higher percentage of moisture.

- Baking Time: The longer a loaf of bread bakes, the more moisture it will lose.

- Oven Temperature: The hotter the baking temperature, the shorter the baking time, thus, the less moisture the bread will lose.

Steam

Commercial bread baking ovens most often will be steam injected. The introduction of steam to the baking environment is beneficial in several ways. The addition of steam to the baking environment cools the surface of the bread allowing enzymes to work longer, which contributes to better crust color. The cooler surface also allows the Oven Spring to proceed without restriction due to early crust formation. Adding steam to the baking environment is only beneficial during the first few minutes of the baking process—no longer than the first 1/3 of the baking time to be sure. One exception to this is with bread that has received an egg wash before baking. These breads do not benefit from steam addition.

Now, with the price tag of a commercial bread oven with steam injection running $45,000 or more, we, as home bakers, will be slow to cough up that kind of cash to bake our sourdough bread. So, can we accomplish nearly the same process? Of course, we can!

A simple way to add moisture to our baking environment is to place a shallow bowl or pan on the bottom rack of our oven and fill it with water before turning the oven on. As the oven temperature rises, so does the water temperature in the bowl/pan. When it reaches 212°F (100°C), it will boil and add steam to the oven baking environment. While this steam addition is not totally under control, it does help the baking conditions of our bread.

Another way is to use a spray bottle adjusted to emit a fine spray of water. I spray the inside of the oven before I put my bread into the oven and then every 5 minutes afterward until the bread has been baking for around 15 minutes. If my bread recipe calls for putting the bread into a cool oven and then set the temperature, I will spray the oven interior every 5 minutes until the oven temperature reaches 212°F (100°C).

Cooling

Once the internal temperature of our bread loaf has reached around 195° to 205°F (90°-95°C), the baking process is complete and the Cooling process begins. From a technical point of view, bread begins to stale the moment it is taken out of the oven and begins to cool. While we always enjoy fresh bread right out of the oven, bread doesn't reach its finest aroma or flavor until it has cooled completely. Sourdough bread, especially, doesn't really come into its own until a few hours after it has cooled. It needs that time for its flavors to settle and mingle. Rye breads made with a high proportion of rye flour, need 24 to 48 hours of resting after the bake to completely develop.

There is, however, a distinction between old bread and stale bread. And, while staling cannot be eliminated, there are ways to prolong the onset of staling and delay the effects of age.

- Cool the loaves carefully — air currents on cooling bread accelerate the evaporation of moisture and can cause a premature crust to form.

- Bread stales more quickly at temperatures between 32° and 50°F (0° to 10°C). We can conclude from this that the worst place to store your bread is in the refrigerator.

- Some people will tightly wrap their bread in plastic and freeze it. Once frozen, the staling process does slow down. But remember, when freezing the bread, it will pass through the danger zone of 32° and 50°F (0° to 10°C) twice — once when lowering the temperature to freeze and again when thawing the bread to room temperature.

- I have found that if I can incorporate some Extra Virgin Olive Oil in my bread recipe, the staling process can be slowed.

Ingredients to Make Bread

I want to take a quick look at the ingredients we use to make bread — at least, the major ones: flour, water, salt, and yeast. I will not go into great detail on this subject as entire books have been written on each of those ingredients. But I do want you to be aware of the profound influence each of these ingredients have on the finished loaf of bread. Once again, if you want more detail on this subject, please refer to Jeffery Hamelman's book.

Flour

Flour obtained from ground grain has been the major food staple for humanity throughout history. There are many different flours derived from many different grains. For the majority of bread recipes, wheat flour is the primary ingredient. In sourdough bread, wheat and rye are the mainstay flours in almost all recipes. But it gets even more complicated than that.

Wheat

I live in an agricultural area of the United States, and wheat is one of the major crops in this area. I can tell you that there is Red Wheat, White Wheat, Hard Wheat, Soft Wheat, Spring Wheat, and Winter Wheat, just to name a few. Each of these wheat variations have a different makeup and properties. Actually, wheat is divided into six (6) categories: 1) Hard Red Winter 2) Hard Red Spring 3) Hard White Winter 4) Durum 5) Soft White Winter and 6) Soft White Spring. The bread baker is most interested in the first four (4) wheat types on the list. I will not go into detail regarding which wheat type is made into which flour; as home bakers we do not need to trouble ourselves with all that information. The choice of flour has been made quite simple to use by the mills. Standing in front of the flour section in your local supermarket, you will usually see the following flour selections: Bleached All-Purpose White Flour, Unbleached All-Purpose White Flour, Unbleached White Bread Flour, Whole Wheat Flour, and Unbleached Whole Wheat White Flour. We will talk about Rye Flour later.

At the mill, after the wheat is ground into flour, it takes three (3) to four (4) weeks for the flour to naturally age (oxidize). Aging is essential to stabilize the baking quality of flour. Flour that is not aged is called "Green Flour" and does not fare well in baking. To avoid the time required to naturally age the flour, a number of chemical additives have been used to artificially mature the flour. Flour that has been chemically bleached requires almost no aging and in as little as a day, is ready for baking.

To bleach flour, a measure of benzoyl peroxide is released into the flour toward the end of the milling process. This whitens and oxidizes the flour. Chlorine gas is also used to bleach flour, but generally only in the milling of cake flour. The chlorine not only whitens the flour but also lowers the pH to around 4.8 which actually improves its ability to properly structure the baked cake.

There are other chemical additives used to artificially age flour — ADA (azodicarbonamide), also known as Maturox, $KbrO_3$ (potassium bromate), and ascorbic acid.

None of this is of any concern to me, as I only use, and recommend using, Unbleached Flour.

There are a few other wheat types—Einkorn and Emmer, Spelt, Kamut, and Triticale.

Rye

Rye grain is of tremendous importance to many parts of Europe. Regardless of the fact that many of America's immigrants arrived from Europe with rye bread recipes in tow, the popularity of rye breads in America has never flourished. Rye bread offers a rich fullness of aroma, a bold flavor, and excellent keeping properties.

Rye flour is significantly different from wheat flour. We must understand these differences apply some unique techniques to be successful with our rye breads. Let's explore some of these differences.

- Remember our mention of the gluten-forming proteins glutenin and gliadin that work "together" to create elastic characteristics as well as resisting characteristics? Due to the presence of Pentosans (we'll discuss Pentosans in a few minutes), gluten formation is not possible. Therefore, rye breads will always have a denser structure than wheat breads.

- Rye flour is higher in bran and fiber than wheat flour, which means rye breads have higher water absorption. Take a pound of water and a pound of wheat flour and mix it, it will resemble pancake batter. Take a pound of water and a pound of rye flour and mix it, it will be much thicker.

- The higher level of bran and minerals in rye also impacts the density of the bread. Bran has a sharp shape and actually cuts the gluten network. Remember, gluten traps the CO_2 which makes the bread rise — if those gluten strands are cut and it can't hold the CO_2, the bread doesn't rise as much, thus resulting in a denser bread. This same process holds true with whole-wheat bread, which is why whole-wheat bread has less volume than white bread.

- Rye has more soluble sugars than wheat, which allows it to ferment more quickly than wheat doughs. While this trait is a benefit when we use rye flour to create new starters, it also means that rye doughs can quickly over-ferment and collapse.

- Rye is high in a substance called "Pentosans" — remember I told you we would talk about this. Pentosans is a polysaccharide substance found in plants and its content in rye flour is higher than in any other flour (around 8%). Pentosans contribute to the high water absorption of rye breads and compete with the glutenin and gliadin in the flour for the moisture. This prevents the development of gluten in the dough. This, and other properties of the Pentosans, requires the mixing of rye dough to be done very gently. Commercial rye bread bakers use a special mixer that turns only 25–40 RPMs, which is only around ¼ the speed of a normal bread mixer.

Sourdough and rye is a match made in heaven. Some of the characteristics of sourdough help the rye bread to develop a properly finished loaf.

Water

Water is a very important ingredient in our bread dough. Some of the factors water contributes are:

- Gluten forms in the presence of water.

- Water is a solvent and dispersing agent for the salt, sugar, and yeast.

- Water is necessary for yeast fermentation.

- Water is responsible for the consistency of bread dough.

- The temperature of water is easily controlled to obtain the proper dough temperature.

- The minerals in water provide food for the yeast which benefits in fermentation.

- Chlorinated water has a negative impact on the yeast culture. If it doesn't actually kill the yeast, it will inhibit the metabolism of the developing microorganisms. Always use non-chlorinated water (or water that has been left uncovered overnight which will allow most of the chlorine to dissipate) in every process of your bread making.

Salt

Salt contributes more to our bread than you would think. Here are some examples:

- Salt adds taste. Bread baked without salt will taste flat. But remember, the role of salt is to enhance the flavor of the bread — not take the place of the true bread flavor.

- Salt tightens the gluten structure which allows it to hold the CO_2 and achieve proper rising.

- Salt retards the activity of the yeast. When mixing your ingredients, try to keep the salt apart from the yeast until either or both of those ingredients are already mixed into the dough. When you use an automatic bread machine (we will discuss the use of the automatic bread machine to make sourdough bread later in this book), make sure you don't place the salt next to or on top of the yeast.

- Salt contributes (slightly) to crust coloring.

- Salt helps preserve the color and flavor of flour.

Yeast

As I mentioned in Part I, when I was in school (and now I'm really going to age myself), they didn't know if yeast was a plant or an animal. It demonstrated characteristics of both. Since then, it has been discovered that yeast is a single-celled microorganism that is a member of the fungus kingdom. Yeast requires several conditions to live and prosper: moisture, oxygen, food, and an appropriate temperature. When those conditions are met, the life cycle of the yeast begins, and it will reproduce and create alcohol and CO_2. This entire process is called "Fermentation" and is the process that the bread baker is interested in using. Yeast is everywhere—floating in the air and collecting on different objects. We will explore this in the section on creating your own starter from scratch. Let's look at those conditions needed by yeast:

- Moisture. Once water is added to the ingredients in your bread dough, the life cycle of the yeast begins. Yeast can only absorb nutrients in a dissolved state, thus it needs water to accomplish this. Also, yeast can only absorb small-molecule nutrients, such as simple sugars through its cell membrane and will release enzymes in order to break down large-molecule nutrients in the dough.

- Oxygen. Oxygen is obtained primarily by the mixing of the dough. Oxygen is required by the yeast for reproduction, but there is virtually no reproduction of yeast occurring in the bread dough. It takes several hours for yeast to begin its reproductive cycle, and there is insufficient time between the mixing of the dough and the baking for reproduction to take place. The exception to this is when we use a pre-ferment (a pre-ferment is where you mix a portion of the overall ingredients and allow it to ferment prior to adding to the final dough mix). We will use the "pre-ferment" method when we cover making sourdough bread in an automatic bread machine.

- Temperature. The discussion of temperature can be very complicated. Correct dough temperature is crucial for yeast activity. Commercial yeast performs best at temperatures between 86° and 95°F (30°–35°C), while wild yeast, the yeast we use for our sourdough bread, has a narrower range of temperature and usually does better at a slightly lower temperature than commercial yeast. I usually shoot for 78°–80°F (25°–27°C) for my sourdough breads. These temperatures are best achieved by the use of a proofing box (see chapter on building a proofing box). At temperatures just above freezing and temperatures around 116°–131°F (47°–55°C), almost all yeast activity stops. At 138°–140°F (60°C), the yeast dies. This is known as the "Thermal Death Point."

- Food. Food is provided to the yeast through the fermentation process, which converts starches into sugar. Yeast cannot directly convert starch to sugar and requires the amylase enzymes naturally present in flour (and may be added at the mill) to convert the starch into fermentable sugars. There is a small amount of sugar naturally present in flour and it is this sugar that is initially consumed by the yeast for fermentation. After the yeast has consumed these sugars, the amylases utilize the damaged starch particles. It is these damaged starch particles that contribute the majority of food to the yeast during fermentation. The whole, undamaged starch particles remain intact in the dough until it reaches the oven, where it becomes available for the other processes in the baking of the bread.

There are a couple of different forms of yeast available to the baker. There is Active Dry Yeast, some form of Rapid-Rise Yeast, and Instant Yeast. Yeast sold under the label of "Bread Machine Yeast" is most likely a rapid-rise type of yeast. I personally use Instant Yeast. Technically, when you use Active Dry Yeast, you should "proof" the yeast. This consists of mixing a little yeast in some water with around a teaspoon of sugar dissolved in the water. In a few minutes, the mixture should start bubbling or foaming. This "proves" that the yeast is viable. However, to be honest, the modern commercial yeasts are of such quality that there is most likely no need to proof it. Instant Yeast can be mixed into the dough without proofing.

Chapter Eleven:
The Proofing Box

What the heck is a "Proofing Box?" The more sourdough bread you create, the more it will become evident that temperature control is very important. When you are developing a new starter, feeding a starter to prepare it to make bread, completing your primary fermentation, and, even, when possible, conducting your final fermentation, it is better not to leave the ambient temperature to the will of the elements, but to have a means to control that temperature.

Instead of using the end table in the family room (the spot I used until I made my proofing box), the top of the refrigerator, or whatever spot you found in your home that maintained the most consistent 78°–80°F (26°–27°C) temperature, a proofing box is the answer to easy temperature control.

Proofing Cinnamon Rolls

Commercial bakers have large, elaborate "proofing ovens" that they can use to proof many loaves of bread at the same time. But, as home bakers, we rarely need to proof more than a couple of loaves of bread at the same time. My home oven has a "proofing cycle" built-in, but after testing the consistency of the temperature provided by this proofing cycle, I found it to be unsatisfactory. It works fine for a couple of hours of proofing, but when creating a new starter, I need around ten (10) days of consistent temperature and, at times, I need to vary that temperature over the fermentation period.

The solution for me was to construct a proofing box. My requirements were that it needed to be large enough to hold my two (2) large glass bowls that I use to work with my starters. That also makes it large enough to hold my baking stone. It also had to be easy to move (although I pretty much leave it in one spot), have a viewing port or be transparent enough for me to see the starters or bread inside, and to not cost an arm and a leg to construct. The picture below is what I came up with to serve as my proofing box. (**Note:** I turned the light off for this photo.)

I will now explain how I constructed my proofing box. Of course, you can choose the specifics of how you want your own proofing box to turn out. It needs to meet your requirements, not mine. But the directions below will serve to point you in the right direction.

Parts Needed to Construct a Proofing Box

I found all of the parts I needed to construct my proofing box at my local hardware store and my local Wal-Mart®. Here is my list of parts:

Light Bulb Receptacle →

Dimmer Switch →

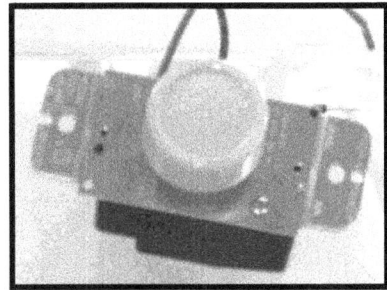

Dimmer Switch Box →

Dimmer Switch Box
Cover →

Assorted Screws and Nuts (not shown in picture)

Electrical Wire
for 110v AC with Plug →

Indoor/Outdoor
Thermometer →

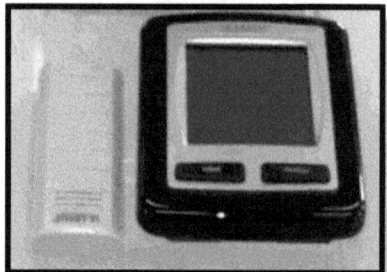

And, of course, the plastic storage container with lid. The photo at the top of the next page shows the container with all the components.

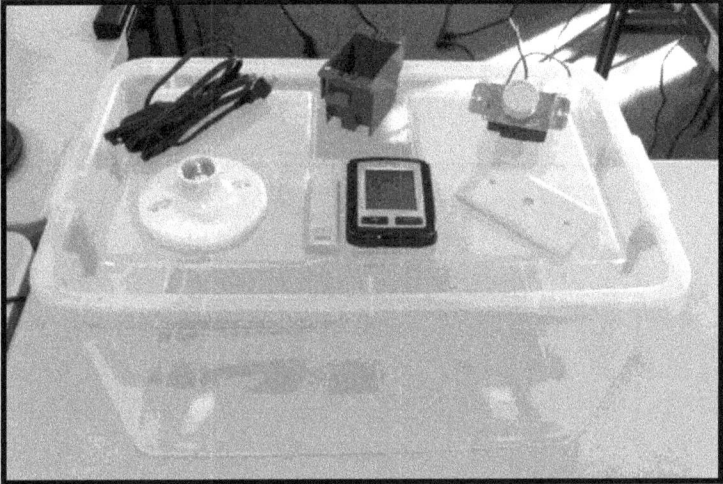

The plastic container is large enough to meet my requirements, and the lid just sits on top of the container. The handles will pivot up to secure the lid, but I do not want to secure the lid, as I'm using the lid for the base of the unit with the container sitting on the lid. This allows the container to be lifted off the lid easily and the lid will catch any overflow or accidents in the box.

Building Instructions

When you study the finished proofing box, you can see that the construction is quite simple. Here is the order I followed to complete the proofing box.

1. I first mounted the light bulb receptacle on the bottom of the container (which becomes the top when the container is inverted) with two (2) screws and nuts. I placed the light bulb receptacle centered on the long measurement of the container and towards either the front or the back of the container.

Light bulb receptacle mounted on inside bottom of container.

2. I then mounted the DIMMER SWITCH BOX on the INSIDE of the container with the ADJUSTMENT KNOB on the OUTSIDE. Cutting the thick plastic of the container may give you some trouble. I drilled a large hole in the container and used a hacksaw blade to cut the rectangular hole needed to fit the Dimmer Switch Box Adjustment Knob.

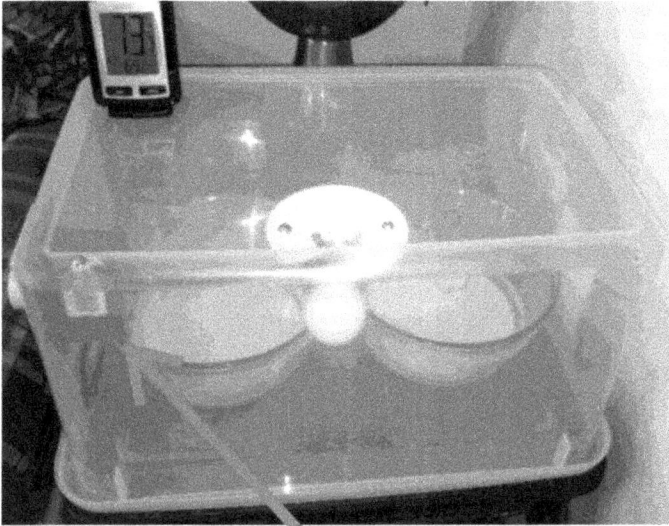

Dimmer Switch Box on inside with knob on outside of container.

3. Wire the light bulb receptacle to the Dimmer Switch and the wire with the plug. Follow the wiring instructions that came with your Dimmer Switch. If you have any doubts, have someone familiar with electrical wiring help you. It is not difficult — one wire from the light bulb receptacle goes to one of the wires with the plug. The other wire from the light bulb receptacle goes to one of the Dimmer Switch wires. The other Dimmer Switch wire goes to the other plug wire. If your wiring has a three-prong plug, you will also have a ground wire. After completing the wiring, mount the Dimmer Switch into the Dimmer Switch Box

and replace the Dimmer Switch Box Cover, mounting it with the screws that came with the Dimmer Switch Box Cover.

4. Mount the Indoor/Outdoor Thermometer transmitter somewhere inside the container.

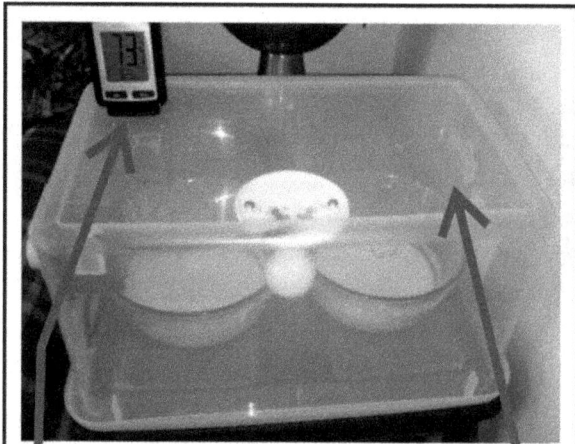

Mount thermometer transmitter on the inside of the container. Mount the thermometer bracket where you can easily see it.

The Indoor/Outdoor Thermometer will come with some kind of mounting bracket—mount that on the outside of the container in a place that will allow you to see the thermometer easily.

5. To test your proofing box, put a light bulb into the light bulb receptacle and plug the wiring plug into a wall socket. Most Dimmer Switches turn on & off by pushing on the control knob.

Turn the Dimmer Switch back and forth to see the light bulb light up and go brighter or dimmer. Now that you know that your Proofing Box works, it's time to calibrate it.

Calibrating the Proofing Box

There are many variables involved with the Proofing Box — the size of the box, the wattage of the light bulb you are using, and the ambient temperature of the room where you have placed your Proofing Box. Ideally, you will be able to put your Proofing Box in a room that stays below 75°F (24°C) most of the time. If the room is warmer than 80°F (27°C), you may have some problems as your Proofing Box cannot cool. If you indeed have a room that stays around 78°F (26°C), you may not have to construct a Proofing Box at all. The room where I have my Proofing Box is a spare bedroom that is almost always below 78°F (26°C).

Once you have found the place for your Proofing Box, let it rest there for an hour or two (2) to stabilize. At this time, your indoor and outdoor temperatures (inside the box/outside the box) should be the same or very close to the same. Start with a very low wattage light bulb in your box. I started with a 15 watt bulb (the kind used in ovens). Plug in the box and turn the dimmer switch to its highest position. Let the box sit for around an hour. Check the temperature inside the box. As I said earlier, many variables contribute to what temperature you will get inside your box. When I used a 15 watt bulb, the temperature didn't increase near enough to use it. I wanted to get a temperature of around 86°-88°F (30°-31°C) with the dimmer switch set to full. I found that I needed a 60-75 watt bulb to accomplish this—your box may work differently. This is why you must calibrate your box. Once you have found the correct wattage bulb for your Proofing Box to get a temperature around 88°F (31°C) on full, then start turning the dimmer switch down a little bit and wait around an hour. Once again, check the temperature inside the box. It should have gone down a little bit. You can mark the knob on the dimmer switch with a Sharpie® and note its location when you turn the knob. Keep doing this until you get a good idea of where you need to turn the knob to get the temperature you want. That's all there is to it.

Once you get used to using your Proofing Box, you will find your bread baking getting more consistent, especially with rising times.

Chapter Twelve:
Creating Your Own Starter

As you know by now, you need at least four (4) things to make bread—flour, water, salt, and yeast. Most bread consumed today is made with these ingredients, plus a few extra ingredients for flavor and consistency. In most cases, highly refined, commercial yeast is used. The modern day yeast you purchase in the supermarket is the result of centuries of specific yeast "breeding" to get a reliable strain of yeast that performs well in a wide range of environments. You can purchase commercial yeast in several forms—yeast cake, dry active yeast, rapid-rise yeast, and even yeast that has been developed especially for use in high-sugar types of dough. These are all wonderful, and I use most of these yeast types on a regular basis.

But I don't always make "regular" bread—often I make my favorite type of bread, sourdough. The yeast used in sourdough bread is "wild yeast" (there are a few exceptions when I use both wild yeast and a little commercial yeast—we will talk about that later).

There are several ways to get wild yeast. You can purchase a yeast culture. There are many places where you can purchase yeast cultures and just as many different styles of yeast cultures. Probably the best known yeast culture readily available is the San Francisco Sourdough Bread yeast culture. These yeast cultures are generally available in a dry powder that you rejuvenate following the instructions that come with the culture. You can also get yeast cultures in a semi-liquid form — kind of like pancake batter, or in a stiff form, kind of like a piece of bread dough. All these forms of yeast cultures will work just fine. I prefer the semi-liquid form as I can easily see what's going on with the starter. As the starter ferments, bubbles form in the "batter." The semi-liquid form of starter is easy to measure and handle, and it stores easily in a 1 quart jar in the refrigerator.

The other way to get your starter is to "create" it yourself. Creating your own starter is fun and gives you insight into how the entire sourdough process works. Now, I must warn you, creating your own sourdough starter takes a bit of commitment to nurture it through its infancy and adolescence to the point where it is ready to make bread. This commitment to time is for eight (8) days with two (2) feedings a day around twelve (12) hours apart. This is not as difficult for me as I am retired (?), but to someone who works a normal job, it does take planning ahead. I generally will feed my starters at 9:00 or 10:00 in the morning and then again at 9:00 or 10:00 in the evening.

Also, creating your own starter does not always end with success. The starter I use most often took me over three (3) months to develop with several disasters along the way. I got starters that made great bread, but it wasn't sour enough to be called sourdough bread. I had a couple of starters that must have gotten infected with some kind of malicious beasts that were out to do me harm. Those went directly into the garbage without passing GO or collecting $200. Among those starters that made great bread but did not fit into the sourdough category, was one I called "Pineapple Express" which was made on a pineapple juice base. The bread it made was light and delicious, but it wasn't sourdough.

There are so many yeast variations all over the world. According to where you live, there could be yeast floating around in the air you breathe that could be developed into a wonderful starter. So, let's get started.

First, let's create a simple semi-liquid starter. To create this starter you will need:

- Whole Rye Flour
- Unbleached White Flour
- Honey
- Water
- Porous Cloth
- A Couple of Glass Bowls
- Plastic Wrap
- Large Rubber Band

Let me expound on the "Porous Cloth" a bit. I use these little cloths sold as dish washcloths. The particular ones I use are called "Scrub Buddies®" and are perfect for my needs. This second picture shows what I mean by being porous. I laid a cloth on top of a quilting template I had laying around. Notice how you can see the template through the cloth.

I imagine you can use a layer or two (2) of cheesecloth, but I think that cheesecloth is a little too porous. The purpose of the porous cloth is to cover your starter at the beginning of its development. You want the air and the airborne yeast to freely flow into the bowl where your starter is, but to also filter out any insects or dirt particles that may be floating around in the air. You will only be exposing the starter to the ambient air for a matter of hours — just long enough for our friendly yeast to fall into the starter. So, here is the step-by-step process of creating your own starter.

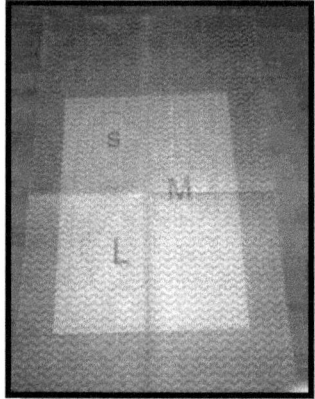

Day One

- 1½ cups whole rye flour – 4.8oz – 136g
- ¾ cup water – 6oz – 170g
- 1 teaspoon honey - .2oz - 5.67g

Mix the ingredients in a medium-size glass bowl. Place your porous cloth on top of the bowl and secure it onto the bowl with a large rubber band.

According to what time of the year you are creating your starter — the best time of the year is spring through fall which usually means 75º–80ºF

(24°-27°C) and a light breeze — place your starter outside where the light breeze can blow over it. Leave it outside for a couple of hours.

Bring your starter inside and remove the porous cloth. Stretch plastic wrap over the top of the bowl and make sure it is sealed well on the bowl. Place the starter in your proofing box with the temperature set to around 80°F (27°C). Let it sit for 24 hours.

Day Two: Two (2) Feedings
Take half of the original starter – 5.5oz – 156g
Discard the rest.

- 3/8 cup whole rye flour – 1.2oz – 34g
- ¼ cup unbleached white flour – 1.2oz – 34gm
- 3/8 cup water at 90°F (32°C) – 3oz – 85g

Mix ingredients and cover with plastic wrap. Place the starter in your proofing box with the temperature set to around 80°F (27°C). Let stand for 12 hours and repeat the feeding process. You may see some bubbles forming.

Days Three through Seven: Two (2) Feedings
Take half of the starter – 5.5oz – 156g
Discard the rest.

- ½ cup unbleached white flour – 2.4oz – 68g
- 3/8 cup water at 90°F (32°C) – 3oz – 85g

Mix ingredients and cover with plastic wrap. Place the starter in your proofing box with the temperature set to around 80ºF (27ºC). Let stand for 12 hours and repeat the feeding process. You should start seeing bubbles forming and smell the wonderful, sour smell of ripening sourdough starter.

If your starter is not producing bubbles by Day Five, you probably don't have a viable starter. I'm almost certain that will not happen, but with sourdough, you never know what it will do. If your starter smells really bad, it is most likely contaminated and needs to be discarded.

Once you have your active starter, follow the directions for Maintaining Your Starter in Part I of this book. Take care of your starter and it will last many, many years.

Collecting Yeast in Other Ways

There is another fun way to create a starter. If you live in an area where wild berries grow, you can actually collect yeast from the surface of the berries. You really need to find a place outside of the city area where the fruit will be more likely to be free of any contamination. I'm fortunate to live outside the city limits and in a very sparsely populated area. We have wild raspberries, blackberries, and the famous berry of Idaho—the huckleberry—readily available to us. If you have someone else collect the berries for you, make sure they do not wash the berries. If you collect the berries yourself, look at the berries as you pick them. Do you see any white powder-like substance on them? That white powder is yeast. You will only need a cup or two (2) of fresh, unwashed berries in order to capture the yeast off of the berries. Take one (1) cup of water and carefully rinse the berries in the water. Save the water. Once you have completely washed the berries in the water, take the one (1) cup of water and measure out ¾ cup to use as the water in your Day -1 starter recipe. It's as simple as that.

Sourdough Rye Culture

Once you have mastered creating your semi-liquid starter and are ready to take on a challenge, try creating a Sourdough Rye Culture. This starter is not a semi-liquid starter, but a much stiffer starter, more like a paste. It acts more like bread dough than the pancake batter — like the starter you have already created.

Here is the procedure:

Day One:

- 1¾ cups whole rye flour – 6.4oz – 181.4g
- ¾ cup water – 6oz – 170g

Mix the ingredients in a medium-sized glass bowl. Stretch plastic wrap over the top of the bowl and make sure it is sealed well on the bowl. Place the starter in your proofing box with the temperature set to around 80ºF (27ºC). Let it set for 24 hours.

Day Two: One (1) Feeding
Take ¼ of the original starter – 3.2oz – 90.7g
Discard the rest.

- 7/8 cup whole rye flour – 3.2oz – 90.7g
- 3/8 cup water at 90ºF (32ºC) – 3oz – 85g

Mix the ingredients in a medium-sized glass bowl. Stretch plastic wrap over the top of the bowl and make sure it is sealed well. Place the starter in your proofing box with the temperature set to around 80ºF (27ºC). Let it set for 24 hours.

Days Three through Nine: Two (2) Feedings
Each day, take 1/3 of the starter – 3.2oz – 90.7g
Discard the rest.

- 7/8 cup whole rye flour – 3.2oz – 90.7g
- 3/8 cup water at 90ºF (32ºC) – 3oz – 85g

Mix ingredients and cover with plastic wrap. Place the starter in your proofing box with the temperature set to around 80ºF (27ºC). Let stand for 12 hours and repeat the feeding process. By Day 6, your starter should be well established. It will rise like bread dough. At this time, you can save the starter normally discarded and start another batch of starter to have as a back-up.

Sourdough Wheat Culture

You can create a sourdough wheat culture if you desire. I usually just use my regular semi-liquid sourdough starter and create a sponge using wheat flour the day before I want to make sourdough wheat bread. But here is the method to create a sourdough wheat starter.

Ingredients

- ½ teaspoon honey
- ½ cup whole wheat flour
- ½ cup non-chlorinated water (such as bottled)

Directions

1. In a glass or ceramic bowl, mix together the honey, ½ cup whole wheat flour, and ½ cup of water. Use a wooden spoon to stir. Cover lightly and place in a warm place. Stir twice a day for 5 days.

2. On the 6th day, mix in ½ cup of bottled water and ½ cup of flour using a wooden spoon. Cover and let stand in a warm place to ferment for 1 day. When you get lots of bubbles and foam on top, you know the starter is active and ready to use.

3. The starter will separate with the flour on the bottom and 'hooch,' a yellow liquid, on top. Just mix well before using or feeding.

4. Store starter in a wide-mouth glass jar. Once refrigerated, the starter only needs to be fed once a week. Use half, and feed the remaining half to keep it alive for the next batch.

Modifying an Existing Starter

Instead of creating a completely new starter from scratch, you can also modify an existing starter to meet your requirements. This is especially true with rye starters. If you don't want to keep a bunch of different starters in your refrigerator, you can modify your existing semi-liquid sourdough starter into a rye starter when you need it for a specific recipe.

For example: Let's say you want to make some sourdough rye bread. Take your semi-liquid sourdough starter and feed it as you do normally. You will then have double the amount of starter available. Take half of this newly-fed starter and put it back in the refrigerator to keep for future bread making. Take the other half of this newly-fed starter and feed it again, only this time, feed it with rye flour (whichever type of starter you need). Your normal feeding mix is 1 cup of Unbleached All-Purpose Flour and ¾ cup warm water. You might want to divide the new feeding into ½ cup of rye flour and ½ cup of Unbleached All-Purpose Flour and ¾ cup warm water. Let it ferment 4-6 hours, then feed it again with the 1 cup rye flour and the ¾ cup warm water. The rye flour will most likely make the starter stiffer. You can add a little more water to the starter when you are ready to use it in bread.

This will allow you to make a custom starter from your existing starter without having to keep different starters in your refrigerator.

I hope these instructions will keep you in starter for the rest of your life. Happy Baking!

Chapter Thirteen:
Making Sourdough Bread in an
Automatic Bread Machine

Have you ever tried to make sourdough bread in an automatic bread machine? If so, you have discovered that it doesn't work all that well. Many sourdough bread recipes that are supposed to be for bread machines use an ordinary bread recipe and add artificial sour flavoring. That's unacceptable.

When I started experimenting with making sourdough bread in my bread machine I found that the rising times programmed into the bread machine were not long enough for sourdough bread. Now, I have to tell you that my bread machine is the Rolls Royce™ of bread machines. It is fully programmable where I can set the rising times long enough to accommodate sourdough. But not everybody has a killer bread machine to work with. So, I limited myself to using a straight white bread course programmed into every bread machine.

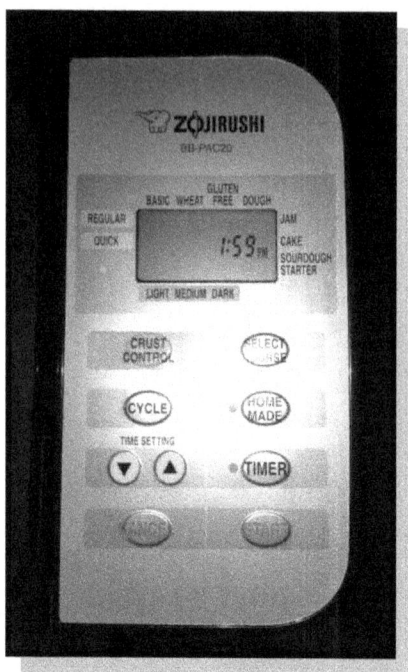

There are a couple of ways to approach making sourdough in a bread machine—both ways incorporate using what we call a "Pre-Ferment." A "Pre-Ferment" is exactly what it sounds like—you mix some of the ingredients together and allow them to ferment. Then you add the balance of the ingredients and go about making your bread.

The first way is to mix the pre-ferment together in your bread machine. Add the balance of the ingredients on top of the pre-ferment putting the flour in first. Set the delay-start on the bread machine for the longest time you can. My bread machine actually sets the delay time to the time you want the bread to be finished, and the maximum time I can set it is 11 hours and 59 minutes. For my machine, that means that the bread machine will start mixing the bread three (3) hours earlier which translates into a nine (9) hour ferment time. Nine (9) hours is not as long as I would like for the pre-ferment, but I have tried it and it works fine — the bread finished perfectly and had a nice sourdough flavor.

The second way to do the pre-ferment is to mix the pre-ferment ingredients in a glass bowl, cover it with plastic wrap, and put it in your proofing box for 12 hours. Once it has pre-fermented, scoop it out of the bowl and put it into your bread machine. Add the balance of the ingredients, and start the machine. If your bread machine has a built-in "Rest" cycle before it starts, and you can de-activate it, do so.

One other thing: to guarantee reliable rising with some consistency, we add a little commercial yeast to the recipe. We are still using our sourdough starter, but we add a little commercial yeast just to smooth out the operation.

Bread machines make different sized loaves of bread, so we have to adjust our bread recipes to accommodate the size loaf your bread machine makes. The Bread Machine Sourdough Bread recipes in this book will make a 2 lb. loaf, 1½ lb. loaf, and a 1 lb. loaf. Here are the recipes:

Bread Machine Sourdough
Yield: One 2lb Loaf – 908 g

Ingredients

¾ cup water + 1 tablespoon – 195 g
3¾ cups bread flour – 480 g, divided into 1¾ cup (224 g) & 2 cups (256 g)
1 cup sourdough starter – 308 g
2 tablespoons sugar – 46 g
2 tablespoons dry milk – 8 g
2 teaspoons salt – 11.2 g
2 tablespoons olive oil – 25 g
2½ teaspoons yeast – 7 g – divided into ½ teaspoon and 2 teaspoons.

Directions

1. Place the starter (308 g) in a large bowl. Add water (195 g) and mix until combined. Sprinkle the ½ teaspoon of yeast on the surface of the starter/water mixture. Add the 1¾ cup (224 g) flour. Mix until thoroughly combined. Scoop the mixture (sponge) into the bread machine pan.

2. Add 2 cups (256 g) flour to totally cover the sponge. Place sugar, dry milk, salt, and olive oil around the edge of the pan. Hollow out a place for the 2 teaspoons of yeast in the dry flour. Add the 2 teaspoons of yeast in that hollow.

3. Set delayed-start timer to 12 hours or the highest time delay your machine will do. This will vary from machine to machine. If your machine has a "Rest" cycle and you can turn it off, do so. Use normal white bread program.

Especially with first attempts, be there to watch the bread mix. Adjust flour or water to get dough at right consistency. If you are using the liquid levain starter (the semi-liquid starter) (3/4 cups water to 1 cup flour), these numbers should be very close.

Optional Method

1. Mix starter (308 g), water (195 g), ½ teaspoon of yeast, and 1¾ cup (224 g) of flour in bowl. Cover with plastic wrap and place in proofing box @ 78°–80°F (26°–27°C) for 12 hours.

2. Stir down sponge and place this sponge into bread machine pan and add other ingredients. If your machine has a "Rest" cycle, and you can turn it off, do so. Set machine for normal white bread program. Hit start.

Bread Machine
Sourdough
Yield: One 1½lb Loaf – 680 g

Ingredients

.5625 cup water + 1½ teaspoons – 147 g
2.812 cups bread flour – 360 g – divided into 1.312 cups (168 g) & 1½ cups (192 g)
¾ cup sourdough starter – 231 g
1½ tablespoons sugar – 35 g
1½ tablespoons dry milk – 6 g
1½ teaspoons salt – 8.4 g
1½ tablespoons olive oil – 19 g
2 teaspoons yeast – 5.6 g – divided into ½ teaspoon and 1½ teaspoons.

Directions

1. Place the starter (231 g) in a large bowl. Add water (147 g) and mix until combined. Sprinkle the ½ teaspoon of yeast on the surface of the starter/water mixture. Add the 1.312 cups (168 g) flour. Mix until thoroughly combined. Scoop the mixture (sponge) into the bread machine pan.

2. Add 1½ cups (192 g) flour to totally cover the sponge. Place sugar, dry milk, salt, and olive oil around the edge of the pan. Hollow out a place for the 2 teaspoons of yeast in the dry flour. Add the 2 teaspoons of yeast in that hollow.

3. Set delayed-start timer to 12 hours or the highest time delay your machine will do. This will vary from machine to machine. If your machine has a "Rest" cycle and you can turn it off, do so. Use normal white bread program.

Especially with first attempts, be there to watch the bread mix. Adjust flour or water to get dough to the right consistency. If you are using the liquid levain starter (3/4 cups water to 1 cup flour), these numbers should be very close.

Optional Method

1. Mix starter (231 g), water (147 g), ½ teaspoon of yeast, and 1.312 cup (168 g) of flour in bowl. Cover with plastic wrap and place in proofing box @ 78-80°F for 12 hours.

2. Stir down sponge and place this sponge into bread machine pan and add other ingredients. If your machine has a "Rest" cycle, and you can turn it off, do so. Set machine for normal white bread program. Hit start.

Bread Machine Sourdough
Yield: One 1lb Loaf – 454 g

Ingredients

.375 cup (3/8) water + 1 ½ tablespoons – 98 g
1 7/8 cups bread flour – 240 g – divided into 7/8 cup (112 g) & 1 cup (128 g)
½ cup sourdough starter – 154 g
1 tablespoon sugar – 23 g
1 tablespoon dry milk – 4 g
1 teaspoon salt – 5.6 g
1 tablespoon olive oil – 13 g
2 teaspoons yeast – 5.6 g – divided into ½ teaspoon and 1½ teaspoons.

Directions

1. Place the starter (154 g) in a large bowl. Add water (98 g) and mix until combined. Sprinkle the ½ teaspoon of yeast on the surface of the starter/water mixture. Add the 7/8 cup (112 g) flour. Mix until thoroughly combined. Scoop the mixture (sponge) into the bread machine pan.

2. Add 1 cup (128 g) flour to totally cover the sponge. Place sugar, dry milk, salt, and olive oil around the edge of the pan. Hollow out a place for the 1½ teaspoons of yeast in the dry flour. Add the 1½ teaspoons of yeast in that hollow.

3. Set delayed-start timer to 12 hours or the highest time delay your machine will do. This will vary from machine to machine. If your machine has a "Rest" cycle, and you can turn it off, do so. Use normal white bread program.

Especially with first attempts, be there to watch the bread mix. Adjust flour or water to get dough to the right consistency. If you are using the liquid levain starter (¾ cups water to 1 cup flour), these numbers should be very close.

Optional Method

1. Mix starter ½ cup (154 g), water (98 g), ½ teaspoon of yeast, and 7/8 cup (112 g) of flour in bowl. Cover with plastic wrap and place in proofing box @ 78-80°F for 12 hours.

2. Stir down sponge and place this sponge into bread machine pan and add other ingredients. If your machine has a "Rest" cycle, and you can turn it off, do so. Set machine for normal white bread program. Hit start.

This recipe makes a very nice loaf of sourdough bread and is easy to do.

Chapter Fourteen:
More Advanced Recipes

In part I, I included a lot of recipes to get the novice started. Now, I also include several more advanced recipes, including some Sourdough Rye Bread recipes.

Honey Whole Wheat
Sourdough Bread

Ingredients:

1½ cups sourdough starter (~390g)
2 cups whole milk (or even water) (~490g)
¼ cup mild honey (85-86g)
2 large eggs
6 cups (divided) whole wheat flour, plus extra for kneading
2 teaspoons sea salt
4 tablespoons vital wheat gluten
6 tablespoons unsalted butter, at room temperature (or coconut oil)

Directions:

1. The night before you are going to bake bread, make a sponge by mixing the starter with the milk and 3 cups of flour. Cover and leave at room temperature overnight, or better yet, in your proofing box set to around 78º–80ºF (26º–27ºC)

2. The next morning, stir the sponge before beginning. Then, add in the honey and eggs, stirring until incorporated. Add the remaining flour, salt, vital wheat gluten, and butter, and use your dough hook to fully mix, then knead for 5-7 minutes, adding more flour as necessary. Don't add too much flour—just barely enough to get the dough pulling away from the sides ever so slightly. This dough is very slack.

   Note: When trying to figure out if you've kneaded enough or added enough flour, keep in mind that developing gluten, the substance in grains that enables a rise, is your goal. "Developed" gluten is sticky and allows you to stretch the bread dough. Elasticity would be a word to keep in mind.

3. Cover the dough with plastic wrap or a towel and put it back in your proofing box. Sourdough takes longer to rise than commercial yeast, so expect to wait anywhere from two to four hours, depending on the strength of the starter. I almost always leave it for four to six, or longer if necessary! Have patience.

4. Butter two 9×5-inch loaf pans. Once the dough has doubled in size, pour it into the loaf pans. Cover the pans again and put them in your proofing box. When the dough has risen at least to the top of the pans or a half-inch above, which takes an hour and a half to three hours,

take your bread out of the proofing box. Position a rack in the middle of the oven and preheat to 375ºF (191ºC).

5. Slash loaves, then immediately bake until they are honey brown and sound hollow when tapped on the top, 35-40 minutes. Use an instant-read thermometer to check the internal temperature of the bread — it should be around 200ºF (93ºC). Be careful not to over-bake this bread or it will be dry. Remove the loaves from the pans and let cool completely on wire racks before slicing.

Sourdough Rye Bread

Ingredients:

1¾ cups water - 400g
1/3 cup sourdough starter - ~70-85g
1¾ cups rye flour - 245g
1¾ cups bread flour - 245g
2 tablespoons molasses - 44g
1 Tablespoon fennel seed - 8g
1 teaspoon anise seed - 2g
1 teaspoon caraway seed - 3g
1¾ teaspoons salt - 12g
Zest of 1 orange

Directions

1. In a mixing bowl, mix the starter into the water. Add the molasses, all the seeds, and orange zest.

2. In a separate bowl, combine the flours and salt.

3. Gradually stir the dry ingredients into the wet, using a dough whisk or spoon, until the flour is well incorporated.

4. Cover with plastic and let rest for 15 minutes. After about 15 minutes, mix again for a minute or two. Again, let rest for 15 minutes and mix one more time as before. Now cover the bowl with plastic and place in your

proofing box set to 78º–80ºF (26º–27ºC) for roughly 12-14 hours.

4. After the long 12-14 hour proof, stretch and fold the dough and shape into boule or batard (round or oblong) shape for baking. Cover again with plastic and let rest 15 minutes before putting in a proofing basket* for the final rise. Place in your proofing box. The final rise should last somewhere between 1 to 1½ hours. Keep the dough covered with plastic to prevent it from drying out.

Note: A proofing basket is not the same as the proofing box. It's just a wicker basket that can be used lined with cloth or unlined to allow the pattern of the wicker to imprint on the dough. (Either way, it must be well-floured first.) However, you need not purchase a special basket for this purpose. If you don't have a proofing basket, line a bowl with a well-floured kitchen towel and put the dough in there for the final rise.

6. Preheat your oven to 475 F (246ºC) a half hour before baking. If you are baking your bread in a covered baker or on a stone, place the baker or stone in the oven while it is preheating.

7. Score the dough with a razor or sharp serrated knife and bake until the internal temp is about 200 F (93ºC). If you are baking your bread in a covered baker, take the cover off around 10–15 minutes before the bake time is completed and finish the bake with the cover off.

Let cool completely before eating.

Sourdough Pumpernickel Bread

Ingredients:

<u>Rye Starter</u>
1 cup sourdough starter (~260g)
1 cup coarse whole-rye flour (~103g)
¾ cup water, room temperature (180g)

<u>Final Dough</u>
2 cups unbleached bread flour (242g)
2 tablespoons brown sugar
1 tablespoon cocoa powder
1½ teaspoons salt
1¼ teaspoons instant yeast
3/4-1 cup breadcrumbs, preferably from rye bread (dry or fresh)
2 tablespoons vegetable oil
¼ cup water, room temperature

<u>For Dusting</u>
Semolina flour or coarse whole rye flour

Directions:

1. The day before making the bread: Mix proofed starter, rye flour, and water in a bowl. This will make a wet, pasty starter.

2. Cover the bowl with plastic wrap and place in your proofing box set to around 78º–80ºF (26º–27ºC) for 4 to 5 hours or until the sponge becomes bubbly and foamy.

3. Immediately put it in the refrigerator overnight.

4. Bread baking day: Remove the rye starter from the refrigerator one hour prior to making the dough.

5. After the chill is off the starter, stir together the flour, sugar, cocoa, salt, and yeast in large mixing bowl.

6. Add the rye starter, bread crumbs and oil and mix on low speed with paddle attachment until the ingredients form a ball.

7. Add additional water if the dough ball does not pick up all the flour, or more flour if the dough seems too wet.

8. With a dough hook attachment, mix on low speed for 4 to 5 minutes.

9. Add more flour as needed to make a smooth, pliable dough ball. It should be tacky but not sticky.

   Note: Rye bread will become gummy if you mix too long, so try to make all adjustments early and minimize the mixing and kneading process.

10. Transfer dough to lightly oiled bowl, rolling it around to coat it with oil.

11. Cover bowl with plastic wrap and ferment at room temperature for 2 hours or until doubled in size.

12. Sprinkle small amount of flour on the counter and carefully transfer the dough to the counter (try not to degas the dough).

13. Divide the dough in 2 equal pieces and shape them into boules or rectangle for sandwich bread.

14. Line baking sheet with parchment (or use proofing basket) and sprinkle with cornmeal, semolina flour or coarse whole-rye flour.

15. If making sandwich bread, lightly oil 8½ by 4 ½ inch bread pan(s).

16. Transfer the dough to the pans, mist the dough with spray oil and cover with plastic wrap.

17. Place in your proofing box at 78º–80ºF (26º–27ºC) for approximately 90 minutes or until the dough crests 1 inch above the lip of the bread pan at the center, or rises to 1½ times its original size.

For Freestanding Loaves:

18. Preheat the oven to 450°F (232ºC), placing a baking stone on the middle shelf and a shallow pan or cast-iron skillet on lower shelf (to provide steam).

19. Score the loaves to allow for expansion.

20. Transfer the dough to the baking stone.

21. Pour 1 cup hot water into the steam pan and quickly close the door.

22. After 30 seconds, open the door and spray the oven walls with water.

23. Repeat twice more at 30 second intervals.

24. After the final spray, lower the oven temperature to 400°F (205ºC) and continue to bake for another 20-30 minutes. Check the breads and rotate 180 degrees, if necessary, for even baking.

25. When done, the bread should register 200°F (93ºC) in the center and sound hollow when thumped on the bottom.

For Loaf Pans:

26. Place pans on baking sheet and place in the oven (middle rack).

27. Bake for 20 minutes, then rotate the sheet pan 180°F for even baking.

28. Continue baking another 20 to 30 minutes or until loaves register 185-195°F (85ºC) in the center.

29. Remove finished loaves from the pan and cool
on a rack for at least 1 hour before slicing.

Glossary

Autolyse
A mixing technique for bread ingredients developed by Professor Raymond Calvel.

Batard
A type of bread shaped similarly to a baguette.

Baguette
Bread in a narrow, oblong shape.

Biga
An Italian word for a pre-ferment.

Bleaching
The process of adding chlorine gas to flour to help oxidize and whiten it.

Boule
A round loaf.

Chlorine
A gas added to flour at the mill to whiten flour. It is also put in city water to kill any "bugs" in the water. Bad for yeast!

Crumb
The inside of a loaf of bread.

Elasticity
The characteristic of bread dough to spring back after being stretched. Gluten contributes elasticity to bread dough.

Fermentation
In bread making, fermentation is the process of yeast converting sugar

into CO_2, alcohol, heat, and organic acids.

Folding	One of the ways to degas bread dough.
Gliadin	A protein in wheat flour that works with glutenin (another protein) to form gluten.
Gluten	The combination of proteins (glutenin & gliadin) that contribute to dough elasticity, extensibility, and strength. It also traps the CO_2 from the yeast during fermentation that causes the bread to rise.
Glutenin	A protein in wheat flour that works with gliadin (another protein) to form gluten.
Lactobacilli	The strains of bacteria produced during sourdough bread production that contribute to the bread's flavor and aroma.
Liquid Levain	Liquid levain is a sourdough leavening agent or bread starter, also known as 'chef.' It is French in origin.
Oven Spring	The rapid rising in bread volume that occurs during the first few minutes of baking.

Pentosans

Pentosans is a polysaccharide substance found in plants and its content in rye flour is higher than in any other flour (around 8%). Pentosans contribute to the high water absorption of rye breads and compete with the glutenin and gliadin in the flour for the moisture. This prevents the development of gluten in the dough. This, and other properties of the Pentosans, requires the mixing of rye dough to be done very gently.

Poolish

A type of pre-ferment made of equal weights of flour and water with a small amount of yeast.

Pre-ferment

A portion of a dough's overall ingredients that are mixed together and allowed to ferment before being added to the final dough mix.

Proofing

A term that means the rising of bread, either before or after loaf shaping. It can also mean testing yeast to see if it is viable.

Proofing Basket

A proofing basket is a wicker basket that can be used lined with cloth or unlined to allow the pattern of the wicker to imprint on the dough. (Either way, it must be well-floured first.) However, you need not purchase a special basket for this purpose. If you don't have a proofing basket, line a bowl with a well-floured kitchen towel and put the dough in there to rise.

Proofing Box   An enclosed area that allows the baker to control the temperature inside the area for precise proofing.

Retarding   The process of slowing down the fermentation by refrigerating the dough.

Sourdough Starter   A culture of microorganisms, sometimes perpetuated over many years, that contains wild yeasts and bacteria. A sourdough culture provides both leavening and flavor to bread.

Sponge   A general term for a pre-ferment.

Starter   A general term for a sourdough culture.

Thermal Death   The temperature at which yeast cells Point (TDP) die—138°F.

Yeast   A single-celled fungus that is used in bread making. It's also used to make beer and wine, although the yeast strains are different. The yeast eats sugar and has CO_2 and alcohol as byproducts.

Index One:
Weight to Volume Conversions

Master Weight to Volume Chart
Common Ingredient Weights & Measures

Item	Measure-ment	Ounces	Grams
Almond Flour, Toasted	1 cup	3 ⅜	96
Almonds, Sliced	½ cup	1 ½	43
Almonds, Slivered	½ cup	2	57
Almond Paste, Packed	1 cup	9 ⅛	259
Almonds, Whole, Raw	1 cup	5	142
Amaranth flour	1 cup	3 ⅝	103
Ancient Grains Blend	1 cup	4 ⅝	131
Apples, Dried, Diced	1 cup	3	85
Apples, Peeled, Sliced	1 cup	4	114
Apricots, Dried, Diced	½ cup	2 ¼	64
Baking powder	1 tbsp	½	14
Baker's Cinnamon Filling	1 cup	5 ⅜	153

Item	Measurement	Ounces	Grams
Bananas, Mashed	1 cup	8	227
Barley, Cooked	1 cup	7 ⅝	216
Barley Flour	1 cup	4	114
Barley, Pearled	1 cup	7 ½	213
Basil Pesto	2 tbsp	1	28
Berries, Frozen	1 cup	5	142
Boiled Cider	¼ cup	3	85
Bran Cereal	1 cup	2 ⅛	60
Bread crumbs(dried, seasoned or plain)	¼ cup	1	28
Bread Crumbs, Fresh	½ cup	¾	21
Brown Rice, Cooked	1 cup	6	170
Buckwheat Flour	1 cup	4 ¼	121
Buckwheat, Whole (kasha)	1 cup	6	170
Bulgur	1 cup	5 ⅜	153
Butter	½ cup or 1 stick	4	114
Buttermilk, Yogurt, Sour Cream	2 tbsp	1	28
Buttermilk powder	2 tbsp	⅞	25

Item	Measurement	Ounces	Grams
Caramel, Individual Pieces	14-16 or ½ cup	5	142
Caramel Bits(Heath™; Chocolate or Chopped Toffee)	1 cup	5 ½	156
Candied Peel	½ cup	3	85
Cashews, Chopped	1 cup	4	114
Cashews, Whole	1 cup	4	114
Carrots, Grated	1 cup	3 ½	99
Cheese, Grated (Cheddar, Jack, Mozz, Swiss)	1 cup	4	114
Cheese, Feta	1 cup	4	114
Cheese, Ricotta	1 cup	8	227
Cheese, Parmesan, Grated	½ cup	1 ¾	50
Cheese Powder	½ cup	2	57
Chickpea Flour	1 cup	3	85
Cherries, Dried	½ cup	2 ½	71
Cherries, Candied	¼ cup	1 ¾	50
Cherries, Frozen	1 cup	4	114
Chives, Fresh	½ cup	¾	21
Chocolate, Chopped	1 cup	6	170

Item	Measure-ment	Ounces	Grams
Chocolate chips	1 cup	6	170
Cocoa, Unsweetened	2 tbsp	³/₈	11
Coconut, Grated, Unsweetened	1 cup	4	114
Coconut Milk Powder	½ cup	2	57
Coconut, Sweetened Flakes	1 cup	3	85
Cookie Crumbs	1 cup	3	85
Coffee Powder	2 tsp	⅛	4
Cornmeal, Whole	1 cup	4 ⅞	138
Corn Syrup	1 cup	11	312
Cornstarch	¼ cup	1	28
Cranberries, Dried	½ cup	2	57
Cranberries, Fresh or Frozen	1 cup	3 ½	99
Currants	1 cup	5	142
Dates, Chopped	1 cup	5 ¼	149
Dough Enhancer and Relaxer	2 tbsp	⅝	18
Egg White, Fresh	1 Large	1¼	35
Egg Yolk, Fresh	1 Large	½	14
Flaxseed	¼ cup	1 ¼	35
Flax Flour	½ cup	1 ¾	50

Item	Measure-ment	Ounces	Grams
Flour Unbleached All-Purpose	1 cup	4 ¼	121
Flour, Bread flour	1 cup	4 ¼	121
Flour, Cake flour	1 cup	4	114
Flour, Unbleached Cake Flour Blend	1 cup	4¼	121
Flour, Gluten-Free Multi-Purpose	1 cup	5 ⅜	153
Flour, Perfect Pastry Blend	1 cup	4	114
Flour, Rice Flour, Brown	1 cup	5 ⅜	153
Flour, Rice Flour, White	1 cup	5	142
Flour, Round Table Pastry Flour (White)	1 cup	3 ¾	106
Flour, Tapioca Flour/ Starch	1 cup	4	114
Flour, Whole Wheat (Traditional)	1 cup	4	114
Flour, Whole Wheat (White)	1 cup	4	114

Item	Measurement	Ounces	Grams
Flour, Whole Wheat Pastry	1 cup	3 ⅜	96
Garlic Cloves, In Skin for Roasting	1 large head	4	114
Garlic, Minced	2 tbsp	1	28
Garlic, Peeled & Sliced	1 cup	5 ¼	149
Ginger, Crystallized	½ cup	3 ¼	92
Ginger Paste	1/3 cup	2 ¼	64
Ginger, Fresh, Sliced	¼ cup	2	57
Graham Crackers, Crushed	1 cup	5	142
Granola	1 cup	4	114
Harvest Grains Blend	½ cup	2 ⅝	80
Hazelnut flour	1 cup	3 ⅛	89
Hazelnuts, whole	1 cup	5	142
Hi-maize®	¼ cup	1 ⅛	32
Honey	1 tbsp	¾	21
Instant Clearjel®	1 tbsp	⅜	11
Jam or Preserves	¼ cup	3	85
Lard	½ cup	4	114
Macadamia Nuts, Whole	1 cup	5 ¼	160

Item	Measurement	Ounces	Grams
Malted Milk Powder	¼ cup	1 ¼	35
Malt Syrup	2 tbsp	1 ½	43
Maple Sugar	½ cup	2 ¾	78
Maple Syrup	½ cup	5 ½	156
Marshmallow Crème	1 cup	3	85
Marshmallow Fluff®	1 cup	4 ½	128
Marshmallows, Mini	1 cup	1 ½	43
Meringue Powder	¼ cup	1 ½	43
Mayonnaise	½ cup	4	114
Milk, Evaporated	½ cup	4 ½	128
Milk, 1%	1 cup	8	227
Milk, Baker's Special Dry	¼ cup	1 ¼	35
Milk, Store Bought Nonfat Dry	¼ cup	¾	21
Milk, Sweetened Condensed	¼ cup	2 ¾	78
Millet, Whole	½ cup	3 ⅝	103
Molasses	¼ cup	3	85
Mushrooms, Sliced	1 cup	2 ¾	78
Oat bran	½ cup	1 ⅞	53

Item	Measurement	Ounces	Grams
Oats, Traditional Rolled or Thick Flakes	1 cup	3 ½	99
Oats, Quick Cooking	1 cup	3 ⅛	89
Oats, Steel Cut, Raw	½ cup	2 ⅞	82
Oats, Steel Cut, Cooked	1 cup	9	255
Oat Flour	1 cup	3 ¼	92
Oil, Vegetable	1 cup	7	199
Olives, Sliced	1 cup	5	142
Onions, Baking	½ cup	1 ⅜	39
Onions, Fresh, Diced	1 cup	5	142
Peaches, Peeled & Diced	1 cup	6	170
Peanut Butter	½ cup	4 ¾	135
Peanuts, Whole, Shelled	1 cup	5	142
Pears, Peeled & Diced	1 cup	5 ¾	163
Pecans, Diced	½ cup	1 ⅞	53
Pineapple, Dried	½ cup	2 ½	71
Pie Filling Enhancer	¼ cup	1 ⅝	46
Pine Nuts	½ cup	2 ½	71
Pistachio Nuts	½ cup	2 ⅛	60

Item	Measure-ment	Ounces	Grams
Pistachio Paste	¼ cup	2 ¾	78
Popped Corn	4 cups	¾	21
Poppy Seeds	2 tbsp	¾	21
Polenta (Coarse Ground Cornmeal)	1 cup	5 ¾	163
Potato Flour	¼ cup	1 ⅝	46
Praline Paste	½ cup	5 ½	156
Pumpkin, Canned	1 cup	9 ½	270
Quinoa Flour	1 cup	3 ⅞	110
Quinoa, Whole	1 cup	6 ¼	177
Quinoa, Cooked	1 cup	6 ½	184
Raisins, Loose	1 cup	5 ¼	160
Raisins, Packed	½ cup	3	85
Raspberries, Fresh	1 cup	4 ¼	121
Rhubarb, Fresh, Medium Dice	1 cup	4 ¼	121
Rice, Long Grain, Dry	½ cup	3 ½	99
Rye Flakes	1 cup	4 ⅜	124
Rye Flour, Medium Rye	1 cup	3 ⅝	103
Rye Flour, Pumpernickel	1 cup	3 ¾	106
White Rye	1 cup	3 ¾	106
Scallions, Sliced	1 cup	2 ¼	64

Item	Measurement	Ounces	Grams
Sesame Seeds	½ cup	2 ½	71
Semolina	1 cup	5 ¾	163
Shallots, Peeled & Sliced	1 cup	5 ½	156
Signature Secrets	¼ cup	⅝	18
Sorghum Flour	1 cup	4 ⅞	138
Sour Cream	1 cup	8	227
Soy Flour	¼ cup	1 ¼	35
Spelt Flour	1 cup	3 ½	99
Sugar, Granulated, White	1 cup	7	199
Sugar, Confectioners' Unsifted	2 cups	8	227
Sugar, Dark or Light Brown, Packed	1 cup	7 ½	213
Sugar, Demerara	1 cup	7 ¾	220
Sugar, Sticky Bun	1 cup	3 ½	99
Sugar Substitute: Splenda®	1 cup	⅞	25
Sugar Substitute: Clabber Girl Sugar Baking Replacer	1 cup	5	142

Item	Measure-ment	Ounces	Grams
Sundried Tomatoes (Dry Pack)	1 cup	6	170
Sunflower Seeds	¼ cup	1 ¼	35
Tahini Paste	½ cup	2 ½	71
Tapioca Flour	1 cup	4	114
Tapioca, Quick-Cooking	2 tbsp	¾	21
Teff Flour	1 cup	4 ¾	135
Toffee Chunks	1 cup	5 ½	156
Vegetable shortening	¼ cup	1 ¾	50
Walnuts, Whole	½ cup	2 ¼	64
Walnuts, Chopped	1 cup	4	114
Walnuts, Water	1 cup	8 ½	240
Wheat Bran	½ cup	1 ⅛	32
Wheat, Cracked	½ cup	2 ⅝	74
Wheat Flakes, Malted	¼ cup	1	28
Wheat Germ	¼ cup	1	28
Yeast, Instant	2 ¼ teaspoons	¼	7
Yogurt	1 cup	8	227
Zucchini, Shredded	1 cup	8 ¼	234

Note: I have not tested all of these items. There are items on this list that I don't even know what they are. It came from a reliable source, but as we know, volume measurements have room for error. Please use these numbers with caution until you know they are dependable

Index Two:
Suppliers & Additional Resources

Suppliers of Books, Starters, Recipes, Etc.

Arm Chair World: Books, Supplies, Kits & Tools
http://www.armchair.com/store/gourmet/starter1.
html

Cultures for Health: Books, Supplies, Starters & Tools
http://www.culturesforhealth.com/sourdough-
baking-supplies.html

King Arthur Flour Company: Books, Supplies, Recipes, Bakeware, Classes & Blog
http://www.kingarthurflour.com/

Sourdough Home: Books, Starters & Recipes
http://www.sourdoughhome.com/

Sourdough International: Books, Starters & Recipes
http://www.sourdo.com/

Books I Recommend

"Bread: A Baker's Book of Techniques and Recipes" By Jeffrey Hamelman

"Classic Sourdoughs: A Home Baker's Handbook, Revised" By Ed and Jean Wood

More From:
The Dramatic Pen Press
www.TheDramaticPen.com

The Sixth Hour
Book I of the Holy Land Mysteries Series
By S. E. Thomas

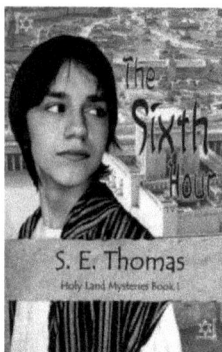

Can Darash, a Jewish teenager, track a killer, rescue his family from ruin, and discover the truth about Yeshua? The rebel, Yeshua, drove the merchants and moneychangers from the Temple with a whip. Hours later, one of them was murdered. Now fifteen-year-old Darash must find a way to protect his family from poverty even as he struggles with the grief of losing his father. When another murder is committed, Darash finds himself searching for a dangerous killer and relying on an old, blind basket-weaver for help. Despite the odds, Darash discovers he has strength of character, a deep compassion for others, and an uncanny knack for problem-solving. But will he be able to expose the killer before the killer finds him? Available in paperback ($13.95) or eBook ($5.99 from Kindle or Nook.)

The Holy Land Mysteries Series
Darash's adventures continue with…
Book II: The Brazen Altar
Book III: The Mud Flower
Book IV: The Leper's Gift
Book V: The Weeping Place
And More!

The Scrolls of the Nevi'im Series

By S. E. Thomas
The prophets of the Old Testament come alive with...

Book I: Habakkuk's Plea: A Prophet of Elohim

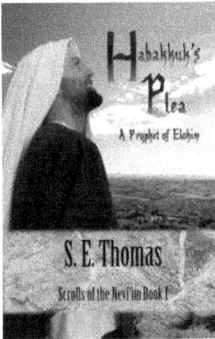

A prophet of God should have answers. Habakkuk has only questions ... questions wrought from sorrow, suffering, and night visions of evil.

When Habakkuk is asked to take in a young refugee—accused of murder—Habakkuk immediately worries about what this will mean for his family of girls. How can he protect them if he brings the enemy under his own roof? But Habakkuk soon discovers an even greater evil residing in the hearts of his kinsmen. Can one man convince a nation to set aside their love of foreign idols and fear the One God alone?

Book II: Habakkuk's Plea: Evil Persists

Though he tries to convince the people to turn to Elohim, they will not listen. Will Habakkuk find a way to reach them before it's too late?

Elohim is testing his heart, testing his compassion. Habakkuk must learn to love the people he is called to serve. But when someone close to him dies, he cries out in agony, "O LORD, how long shall I cry, and You will not hear?" Will Elohim give Habakkuk the answer he longs for? Or is this only the beginning of his test of faith?

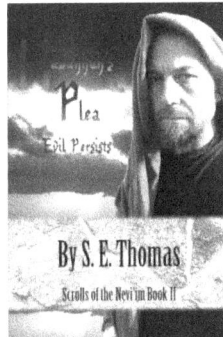

Book III: Habakkuk's Plea: Elohim Answers

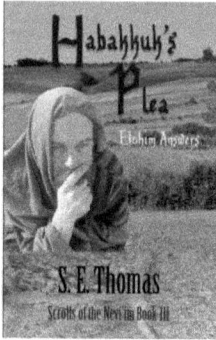

His land will be sacked and burned, his countrymen killed and exiled. How can Habakkuk place his faith in a God who allows such suffering?

Warned by a terrifying vision, the prophet Habakkuk knows only one end awaits—the destruction of Judah. It falls to him to warn the People of impending disaster, but can he overcome his own struggle to understand the God he serves? As the Babylonian hoards descend upon them, as death and exile threaten his wife and daughters, will Habakkuk's God remember mercy?

Longing for Rest
A Novella
By S. E. Thomas

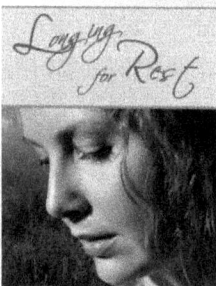

One heartbroken woman battles insomnia. Another cannot escape the coma trapping her between dreams and reality. Though they have never met, through a miraculous crossing of consciousness, they find themselves together on a grassy hill surrounded by a mysterious fog. In this dream world, Amy and Gracie form an unusual friendship. But will fear, pain, and betrayal follow them and spoil this haven? Will they finally be able to rest? Can a dream change your life? Available in paperback ($7.99) or eBook ($2.99 from Kindle or Nook.)

Longing for Rest's Companion Novella
Angel's Choice
Coming Soon!

Be Inspired by Poetry
from Montana Artists of All Ages

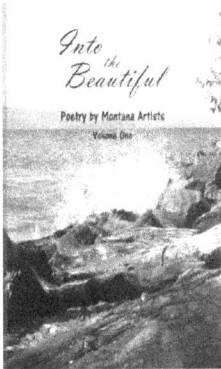

Into the Beautiful
Poetry by Montana Artists
Volume One

"Into the Beautiful: Poetry by Montana Artists" (Vol.1, 2015) is a collection of poetry by Montana artists of all ages. These works of art and creativity were collected through annual contests run August through October. To find out more about this contest, please visit our website at www.thedramaticpen.com.

Throw a Mystery Party!

Who Invited The Stiff to Dinner?
An Interactive Party Game for Teens and Adults
By S. E. Thomas

The guests arrive for a distinguished dinner party at the wealthy English estate of Richard Orwell Mortice. But why would he invite so many of his enemies into his home, along with a Scotland Yard Inspector? When the maid discovers good ol' Rick O. Mortice dead, the Inspector and his overly eager Lieutenant sidekick are out to discover the culprit! Everyone has a motive, and the accusations fly—but not before they go ahead and sit down to a luxurious meal. After all, why let one stiff ruin dinner? *(Requires 15 participants. Includes full, reproducible script, invitation templates, nametags, place settings, and a full set of host/hostess directions. Templates available online for free download.)*

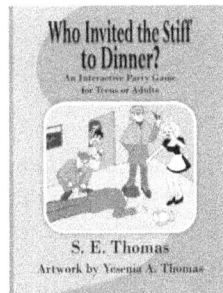

Murder at Surly Gates
An Interactive Party Game for Teens and Adults
By S. E. Thomas

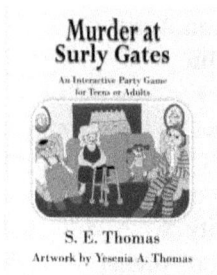

**Murder at
Surly Gates**
An Interactive Party Game
for Teens or Adults

S. E. Thomas
Artwork by Yesenia A. Thomas

Tensions are high when the cantankerous residents of Surly Gates Nursing Home have to put up with money-hungry relatives, a spoiled brat, and her incompetent mother during visitors' hours. When the nursing home manager turns up dead in his office, everyone is a suspect! Who had something to gain from his death? What happened to Badger's heart pills? Why does Lily, a former beauty queen, still try to swing her hips—even behind her walker? Buster, a resident and former security guard, and his son, Doyle, a bumbling cop, want to solve this case! *(Requires 15 participants. Includes full, reproducible script, invitation templates, nametags, place settings, and a full set of host/hostess directions. Templates available online for free download.)*

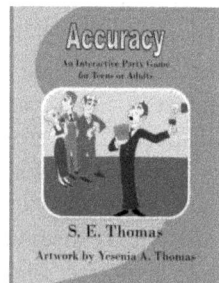

Accuracy
An Interactive Party Game for Teens and Adults
By S. E. Thomas

A successful, but pompous, author is murdered on the night of his new book debut celebration. A note—intended to stop the murder—actually spurns the killer into action due to some rearranged punctuation. Who wrote the note? Who tampered with the note? Who carried out the false instructions? Nearly everyone has a motive! An intelligent Spanish lawyer with a very thick accent discovers the truth. *(Requires 11 participants. Includes full, reproducible script, invitation templates, nametags, place settings, and a full set of host/hostess directions. Templates available online for free download.)*

Accuracy
An Interactive Party Game
for Teens or Adults

S. E. Thomas
Artwork by Yesenia A. Thomas

Let Them Eat Cake
An Interactive Party Game for Teens or Adults
By S. E. Thomas

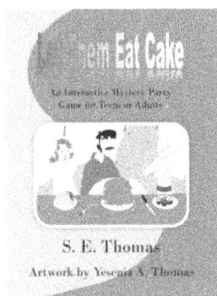

A reputable cake-baking contest is underway and the contestants are vying to win 20% of the stock in the wealthy contest sponsor's restaurant business. Then the sponsor turns up dead! He ate an entire cake ridden with arsenic-bearing apple seeds! Who gave him the cake? Who wanted him dead? Why in the world didn't he stop at the first bite? A bumbling security guard who is allergic to flour is on the case! *(Requires 14 participants.)*

A Full-Length Christmas Production for Your Church or Christian School!

A Reason To Celebrate
A Full-Length Christmas Production
By S. E. Thomas

For most, Christmas is a time filled with joy. But for many, Christmas can be a difficult season. Some may even feel Christmas is not a time of celebration, but of sorrow…. But let us consider a moment what Scripture tells us of the first Christmas. For the first time, God Himself—the Creator of the Universe, the King of Kings, the Everlasting Father—stepped into our world! He stepped in—not to enjoy the wealth or the beauty or the joys—but to experience our suffering, our longings, and our sorrows. And, even from the moment of His birth, He experienced far from ideal circumstances. And yet, we remember His words, "In this world you will have trouble. But take heart! I have overcome the world."

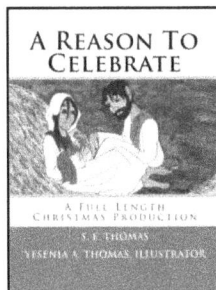

Soon to Come!

THE GALAXY TRILOGY
Enter a dystopian future of terror and adventure with…

Book I: Force Down the Night

Book II: The Third Underground

Book III: Sixteen Digits

Acting Out Loud
Christian Skits and Dramatic Readings
By S. E. Thomas

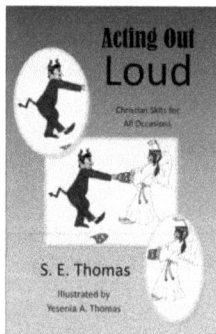

Whether you are a pastor looking for a skit to help really drive home your message, a ministry leader looking for a dramatic reading to speak God's love at a Christian retreat or conference, or a youth group leader wanting to spice up a youth meeting, we have the material you're looking for! This book offers Biblical skits, skits dealing with issues relating to the Christian walk, evangelistic skits, skits for special events, and holiday skits. Now your audience can experience what it's like to wait their turn in the Hades Complaint Department, learn how to bless others from the Fastest Tongue in The West, or get a glimpse into the hectic life of a pastor through these dramatic presentations that, while fun and entertaining, also deliver a powerful, godly message.

Please Visit Us Again!

Find books, plays, skits, mystery party games, fundraising resources, free downloadable program templates, writers' resources, and much more at:

www.TheDramaticPen.com

Write To Bless The World

www.ingramcontent.com/pod-product-compliance
Lightning Source LLC
Chambersburg PA
CBHW071339090426
42738CB00012B/2939